PIERS PLOWMAN

A Facsimile of the Z-Text in Bodleian Library, Oxford, MS Bodley 851

ALSO PUBLISHED

Piers Plowman: A Facsimile of
Bodleian Library, Oxford, MS Douce 104
introduced by Derek Pearsall, and
with a catalogue of the illustrations
by Kathleen Scott

PIERS PLOWMAN

A Facsimile of the Z-Text in Bodleian Library, Oxford, MS Bodley 851

introduced by
CHARLOTTE BREWER
and
A. G. RIGG

D. S. BREWER

First published 1994
D. S. Brewer, Cambridge

ISBN 0 85991 396 1

D. S. Brewer is an imprint of Boydell & Brewer Ltd
PO Box 9, Woodbridge, Suffolk IP12 3DF, UK
and of Boydell & Brewer Inc.
PO Box 41026, Rochester, NY 14604–4126, USA

British Library Cataloguing-in-Publication Data
Langland, William
Piers Plowman. – Facsimile of the Z-text in Bodleian Library, Oxford, MS Bodley 851. – facsim.ed
I. Title II. Brewer, Charlotte III. Rigg, A. G.
821.1
ISBN 0–85991–396–1

Library of Congress Cataloging-in-Publication Data
Langland, William, 1330?–1400?
[Piers the Plowman]
Piers Plowman : a facsimile of the Z-Text in Bodleian Library, Oxford, MS Bodley 851 / introduced by Charlotte Brewer and A.G. Rigg.
p. cm.
Includes bibliographical references.
ISBN 0–85991–396–1
1. Langland, William, 1330?–1400? – Manuscripts – Facsimiles.
2. Manuscripts, English (Middle) – England – Oxford – Facsimiles.
3. Christian poetry, English (Middle) I. Brewer, Charlotte, 1956– .
II. Rigg, A. G. III. Bodleian Library. Manuscript. Bodley 851.
IV. Title.
PR2010.B7 1994
821'.1–dc20 93–38899

This publication is printed on acid-free paper

Printed in Great Britain by
St Edmundsbury Press Ltd, Bury St Edmunds, Suffolk

Contents

The publishers are grateful to the Bodleian Library, Oxford,
for permission to reproduce MS Bodley 851,
fos. 5r–v, 6v and 124r–140v

The folios are reproduced at 87% of their original size

The Z-Text of Piers Plowman

CHARLOTTE BREWER

The version of *Piers Plowman* found in Bodley 851 played no part in *Piers Plowman* studies, whether early or late, until 1873, when Walter Skeat wrote about it in his edition of the C–Text for the Early English Text Society.* Skeat came across the MS towards the end of his great editing enterprise, and consequently named it Z. His dismissive judgement on the early part of the version was perhaps responsible for its continuing almost entirely neglected for the next hundred-odd years. In 1983, this peculiarly truncated version of the poem was edited for the first time by A.G. Rigg and the present writer. We argued that Z represented a copy of an authorial draft of *Piers Plowman*, antedating the composition of A, B and C, a hypothesis which was fiercely resisted by George Kane, the poem's major twentieth-century editor.[1]

The subsequent controversy can be reduced to two basic positions: either one believes, with Kane, that the evidence of the *Piers Plowman* MSS points to the existence of three original versions of the poem and three only, and that the enormous diversity in the MSS is attributable to scribal corruption, or one is prepared to tolerate the notion of 'rolling revision' of the poem, assuming that the author may have produced more than three versions, and that the MS diversity may therefore be attributable to authorial as well as scribal re-writing of the poem. Decision between these two alternatives necessitates a close scrutiny of editorial principles and techniques, and it is particularly important to look back at the origins of our present textual views of the poem. Only then can we place Z in an intelligible historical and taxonomical context.

Piers Plowman survives in the most complex MS tradition to be found in a Middle English poem. Early in the poem's transmission, scribes seem to have recognized that different lengths and types of the work were available, combining shorter with longer versions.[2] The question of what constitutes an A–, B– or C–Text, and the status and validity of these versions – can we really say they

* *Acknowledgements*. I am grateful to the librarians of Cambridge University Library, Kings College London and University College London for permission to quote from MSS and papers held in their collections.

1 George Kane is editor-in-chief of the Athlone Press edition of the poem, which has so far appeared in two volumes (Kane 1960, and Kane and Donaldson 1975). An edition of the C–Text by George Russell is forthcoming.

2 For a list of conjoint MSS, see Kane 1988, 179–80.

are authorial, or do they represent editorial constructs, whether modern or medieval? – are obviously crucial in any evaluation of the unconventional text of the poem found in Z. The terms A, B and C was first used by Walter Skeat in 1867 (xiii), and were immediately adopted by scholars and critics; but the research underlying his identification of three different original versions of the poem had begun long before.

The poem was first published in 1550, by Robert Crowley, in an edition so popular that it was reprinted twice in the same year. The three impressions vary textually, and it seems that Crowley knew of at least four different MSS: two (or possibly three) B versions, on which his edition was largely based, and one MS each of A and C (Kane and Donaldson 7, King 328–29). During the two hundred and fifty years before the next edition, various textual scholars and antiquarians made educated guesses about the likely evolution of the poem. As early as 1725, Thomas Hearne was 'certain that this work of Pierce Plowman's visions hath been much altered at different times', and suggested that it had been subject to authorial revision.[3] Thomas Tyrwhitt suggested in his 1775 edition of *The Canterbury Tales* (vol. 4, 74–75 n. 57) that textual corruption had played a significant part in the transmission of *Piers Plowman*, commenting that Crowley's text had 'been printed from so faulty and imperfect a Ms. that the Author, whoever he was, would find it difficult to recognize his own work'. A third scholar, Joseph Ritson, had clearly identified two separate versions of the poem by 1802: that found in Crowley's edition and in several A– and B–MSS known to him, and that found in various British Museum C–MSS (Ritson, 26–31). Had he compared the A– and B–MSS together in more detail, he would presumably have realised that they represented more than one version of the poem.[4]

Several years later, in 1813, the Lancashire vicar Thomas Dunham Whitaker produced an edition of the C–Text, based on MS Hm 137 (*olim* Phillipps 8231). Whitaker seems to have been more aware than Crowley of the differences between the various versions, but again neither he nor the next editor, Thomas Wright, who published an edition of the B–Text in 1842, read through the MSS known to them in their entirety, and perceived the full degree to which one version could differ from another. Whitaker had looked at two other MSS besides Hm 137: a mixed version of A, B and C (Hm 114, *olim* Phillipps 8252), and a B–MS (Oriel College Oxford 79). He was also familiar with Crowley's text. Whitaker believed that his C–MS represented the poet's first version of the poem, and that the shorter versions found in Crowley's edition, in the Oriel B–MS and in Hm 114 were copies of later revisions. His chosen

3 Hearne's edition of Robert of Gloucester's *Chronicle* makes it clear that he believed three separate versions of both this work and *Piers Plowman* had originally existed. See DiMarco 124–9.

4 See DiMarco 128–9, for a suggestion that Ritson did guess of the existence of three versions of the poem.

C–MS abounded with 'Saxon words and idioms, which in succeeding transcriptions, at a period when the English language was undergoing a rapid change, were gradually removed, with many original passages, which the greater maturity of the author's judgement induced him to expunge' (xxxi). This judgement would now be discounted, on the grounds that Whitaker's views on the poem's language are mistaken, but it is interesting to observe his assumption that an author would cut his work as he revised rather than add to it. There is no reason why this should not be the case, although editors of the poem have always subsequently supposed – rarely arguing the case – that the author progressively expanded his work.[5] Other of Whitaker's assumptions are also notable, although neglected or scorned by subsequent editors. For example, he is clear that authorial revision did not necessarily imply authorial improvement, any more than it necessarily implied authorial expansion: he imagines the poet at work in his study, 'sedate and thoughtful, yet wildly inventive, digesting the first rude drafts of his Visions; and in successive transcriptions, as judgment matured, or invention declined, or as his observations were more extended, expanding or contracting, improving and sometimes perhaps debasing his original text' (vi). At this early stage in editing the poem, it is possible for editors to entertain a range of exploratory notions about how it was composed and what the various MSS represented. Later, after the pioneering work of Skeat had established a virtual orthodoxy, it would be much harder to diverge from the standard view.

Whitaker's edition was unsatisfactory for several reasons. The black letter type probably made it less than accessible to some readers; while the text itself was transcribed from the MS with marked inaccuracy, rendering a good deal of it unintelligible. Thomas Wright recognized the inadequacy of Whitaker's work and produced another edition thirty years later, this time based on a B–MS (Trinity College Cambridge, B.15.17).[6] He dismissed Whitaker's theory that the Phillips MS contained the original version of the poem, arguing instead that the Trinity MS was 'the best and oldest manuscript now in existence' (Introduction, 2nd edn, xxxix). He knew of many more MSS than Whitaker, and believed they constituted two main types, as represented by Whitaker's and Crowley's texts respectively (xxxiii).[7] Wright also knew of an A–MS, Trinity College Cambridge R.3.14, to which he refers several times in his notes, very

5 See Kane and Donaldson 72–74, and n. 13 below.

6 See the article in *Gentleman's Magazine* 1 (1834) 385–91, probably by Wright, for a critique of Whitaker's work; and see also Wright's remarks on Whitaker in the Introduction and notes to his own edition of the poem (*passim*).

7 This statement indicates a failure to collate his various sources of information, both medieval and contemporary: in fact, Richard Price, whose 1824 edition of Thomas Warton's *History of English Poetry* Wright knew and referred to, had already suggested that *three* separate versions of the poem could be identified: the third represented by one of the Harley MSS in the British Library (Harley 6041, or H^2). See Warton 101–2, 478, 481–510. Wright refers to Price's edition in his note to line 453 of his text. Wright's often faulty performance

occasionally inserting the odd reading or line into his text and more often quoting in his notes a line or passage that differed from his own or Whitaker's text.[8] But he nowhere gives any indication that it differs materially from the other two versions.

The first three editors, then, evince varying degrees of awareness of the textual complexity of MS relations, and hazard a variety of off-the-cuff theories and opinions as to the originality and authenticity of the MSS they choose to consult. There was a general consensus that the author revised his text, and also that a significant amount of scribal corruption had occurred.

The next editor to turn his attention to *Piers Plowman*, Walter William Skeat, transformed our understanding of the poem. Skeat came to editing by a somewhat circuitous route. He read mathematics at Christ's College, Cambridge, was made a Fellow in 1860, and in the same year married and became ordained. But he was forced to retire from the priesthood a couple of years later, owing to a throat infection, and returned to Cambridge where he took up a lectureship in mathematics at his old College.[9] As it happened, it was in the following year, 1864, that Frederick J. Furnivall set up his new project, the Early English Text Society. Casting around for prospective editors, he alighted on Skeat as 'one who was fond of Early English and had some leisure'. Skeat embarked on an edition of *Piers Plowman* as his second editorial venture, beginning work in 1866 and publishing the last of its several volumes in 1886.[10] Given his almost amateur status, the speed with which he produced his substantial editions was phenomenal, especially considering that he published a substantial amount of other material at the same time. His EETS edition of A appeared almost immediately, in 1867, followed by B in 1869 and C in 1873. Two separate volumes of notes and glossary were published in 1885. Then in 1886 the Clarendon Press published Skeat's three texts together, in a two-volume parallel-text edition. The first volume contained the texts of the poem, arranging the three versions side by side across each double-page spread, thus making it much easier for the reader to compare and contrast the three versions. The second volume contained notes and glossary. It was this edition of the poem that became the best-used scholarly one – for obvious reasons: the utility of the parallel lay-out and the comparatively uncumbersome format of two volumes rather than five. But the consequences of this scholarly preference were not insignificant for determining views on the poem's textual origins. For example, the two-volume edition has much less information on the characteristics of the MSS than the previous editions, and it does not spell out clearly and fully Skeat's editorial principles and practice. Hence the provisional

as an editor was well recognized during his lifetime as well as subsequently; see e.g. Garnett 1848, 319.

8 The second Trinity MS contains a version of the A–Text followed by a C continuation.

9 See the autobiographical sketch in Skeat 1896, xx–xxi.

10 He had edited only *Lancelot de Laik* (Skeat 1865) before.

character of his A–Text, and the sporadic nature of Skeat's collation of many of the MSS, are not clearly evident from a reading of the parallel-text edition alone.[11]

It is important to bear in mind Skeat's lack of editorial experience when he embarked on *Piers Plowman*, even though he tackled the problem of editing the poem in a much more scholarly and professional way than any of his predecessors. His task was an overwhelming one. None of the previous editors had established with any degree of thoroughness or accuracy what the relationships between any of the MSS were, or how these related to the work that the author (or authors) had (presumably) written in the first place. Reading through the introductions to Skeat's successive editions, one receives an impression of how his perceptions, insights, and assumptions about the poem and its various stages gradually accumulated, and it becomes easier to understand why his judgement on the Z–Text was so uncompromisingly condemnatory.

Skeat knew that a large number of differing MSS of the poem existed, and he fully appreciated that the first task in editing was to trace as many of these as possible. This was a significant advance in editorial method where *Piers Plowman* was concerned.[12] The information Skeat gives us on the inception of his edition relates principally to MS identification and clarification, and he describes how he and Furnivall circulated a short passage from Passus III of the poem among the librarians of Oxford, Cambridge and elsewhere as a means of identifying all known MSS of the poem. The passage was assumed, on obviously *a priori* grounds, to be a distinguishing characteristic of a *Piers Plowman* MS. As we shall see, this was a significant assumption, for it ruled out Z as a qualifying version of the poem. The fruits of this exercise took the form of a pamphlet (or as Skeat called it, a tract), no. 17 in the Early English Text Society series, entitled *Parallel Extracts from Twenty-nine Manuscripts of Piers Plowman, with Comments, and a proposal for the Society's three-text edition of this poem* (1866). The intention was to elicit information on the whereabouts of further MSS of the poem from EETS members and readers, so as to produce a subsequent edition of the poem that took into account as much of the extant evidence as possible. Skeat printed parallel extracts from the twenty-nine MSS his initial search had turned up, categorizing them according to the way in which they represented the passage from Passus III and certain other passages. His choice of these passages was necessarily made without a full and extensive knowledge of the various MS versions of the poem: it represented a preliminary organizational foray into uncharted territory. As he describes, he found that

11 The scholarly popularity of the parallel-text edition also makes it easier to understand how the later editors of A, Knott-Fowler and Kane, came to overlook the existence of Bodley 851 when editing A; see further below.

12 Though it was not a new principle in the editing of Middle English texts; cf. Tyrwhitt's statement at the beginning of the Preface to his edition of the *Canterbury Tales* (vol. 1, i).

there were, in the MSS that he had seen, three reasonably separate versions of the poem. Hitherto, two versions only had been identified; but now

> a further separation of the MSS. can easily be made, so as to distribute them not only into *two* distinct classes, but into *three*. A close and careful scrutiny of several MSS. shows that those which most resemble the one printed by Mr Wright can be separated into two kinds, which may very conveniently be named the *Vernon* and *Crowley* types. The first of these is best exemplified by the text of the Vernon MS. at Oxford, and it is remarkable as presenting the earliest or original version of the poem. It is easily recognized by observing that it omits many long passages, and, in particular, the one containing the story of the rats in the Introductory Passus. It also contains *very few* Latin quotations, and does not extend much beyond ten *Passus*, though it is sometimes [i.e., in some MSS] supplemented by a later text. Its readings are, in general, peculiarly good, and the sense more simple and distinct than in later versions.

He concludes,

> The *three* texts, then are (1) those of the *Vernon* type; (2) those of the *Crowley* type; and (3) those of the *Whitaker* type. It is proposed to publish one of each kind in the above order, so as to show the gradual development of the poem from its briefest into its most elaborate form (3–4).

Here one can see taking shape the unargued assumption that the shortest version must precede the longest, and that the poet would have expanded, rather than contracted, as he wrote.[13] Skeat goes on to observe that the 'variations' between the printed texts, Whitaker's C and Wright's B, 'are far more numerous and important than has been supposed' (he lists some of the major examples), and also stresses that 'it is obviously very desirable to ascertain whether all of the MSS. of each supposed type follow the same difference of arrangement, &c.; and whether any new MS. of value can be anywhere discovered. The present tract is put forth in the hope of obtaining further information on these points'.

By the time his A–Text was published the following year, Skeat had made considerable advances in his understanding of the manuscript relations and his hypotheses about the original versions they might be supposed to represent. He has now discovered that 'the poem takes no less than *five* different shapes, but

[13] See also Skeat 1873, xiv–xv. The assumption that A was composed before B and B composed before C has rarely been discussed; for its justification see Kane and Donaldson 72–74 and cf. Rigg and Brewer 12–13. The assumption has recently been questioned by Hudson, 49–60 (see particularly 59–60). Jill Mann has also suggested (in a paper delivered at the 1993 Cambridge Langland Conference) that A might have originated as a teaching text composed *after* B, which would explain its significantly shorter length, the absence of many discursive passages and complex incidents, and its far smaller number of Latin quotations, very few indeed of which are from non-Biblical sources.

two of them are merely owing to differences of arrangement made by the scribes; and there are really no more than three forms of it'; and for the first time he designates the texts A, B and C.[14] He has also discovered Price's note to Warton's *History of English Poetry*, which had suggested as early as 1824 the existence of a text separate from and previous to the two versions printed by Whitaker and Wright.[15] The coming to light of eight additional MSS strengthened Skeat's view that A came before B and B before C: 'we have abundant evidence of its being really the first and original draught of the poem . . . Type B is obviously derived from it almost wholly by amplification and addition, and preserves nearly the same order in the narrative, even when C wanders away from both'. Also, '(which greatly helps the argument) the Latin quotations occurring in A are much fewer than those found in the corresponding parts of B and C, even when all allowance is made for the amplification of the story.' These remarks present a point of view rather than an argument, and many of Skeat's verdicts on the various MSS are similarly arrived at.

The new A–MSS had not, in Skeat's view, displaced the primacy of the Vernon MS as the best representative of text A, and the date of the MS – about 1370–80 – reinforced the view that this text was the first of Langland's three versions, since it was the earliest known of all *Piers Plowman* MSS.[16] But Skeat's description of how he had examined the A–MSS to come to this decision on Vernon may give us pause for thought. The glowing terms in whch he praises Vernon[17] immediately arouse the suspicion that it was the magnificent appearance of the MS as much as its content which recommended it to Skeat, despite his rebuttal of this possible inference: 'This MS. was taken for the text, not solely because it is the oldest and best written, but also because a careful collation of it with the rest has shewn that its readings are, on the whole, better than those of any other. It seems to me the best known MS. of "Piers Plowman" *in every respect*'.[18] Unfortunately, he does not reveal the criteria on which his judgement was based.

Skeat is perfectly straightforward and open about his highly selective use of the MSS, which is interesting in view of the reviews of his work. As time went on, and one edition after another appeared, the combined oeuvre seemed to

14 1867, xii–xiiii. He later settled on *ten* different forms (Skeat 1886, xxii–iii).

15 See note 7 above. Furnivall had known of Price's identification much earlier; on 20 May 1865, he had written in a postscript to a letter to Henry Bradshaw, the librarian of Cambridge University Library and friend and colleague of both himself and Skeat, 'Thos Warton's note says there are 3 versions of P. Plowman. . . .' (CUL Add 2591, no. 250).

16 Skeat 1867, xiv: 'It is also to be noted that the oldest and best MS. yet found, the Vernon MS., belongs to the earliest type [A]'.

17 'This MS. is indeed a noble and admirable one. Its immense size, and the beauty of the vellum, of the writing, and of the illuminated letters have long since attracted notice, and it has already been made considerable use of by editors and several extracts from it are in print' (1867, xv).

18 1867, xvi.

take on a cumulative weight and authority. Critics must have been perfectly well able to consult component parts of the editions and see that Skeat was building hypotheses on sometimes only partly consulted MSS, but no acknowledgement of this appears in their reviews, which are almost without exception overwhelming in their praise, particularly of the comprehensiveness of Skeat's editorial enterprise.[19] In fact, Skeat examined very few of the MSS in any detail. He collated three other MSS in full against the text of Vernon: Harley 875 (H), Trinity College Cambridge, R. 3. 14 (T), which he found 'very remarkable and valuable', and the A–Text in University College Oxford (U). In addition, Skeat drew sporadically upon the readings of three other MSS (Harley 6041 (H^2), Douce 323 (D), and Ashmole 1468 (A)), thus producing an edition based on seven MSS in all. According to his own account, Skeat did not read through the latter MSS thoroughly, dismissing their readings on various (unsatisfactory) grounds: H^2 was 'little else than an inferior duplicate of T, and may be neglected without much loss. Yet it has occasionally been consulted in difficult passages, and readings from it will be found here and there throughout the book'; D was 'full of gross blunders. On this account, after collating with Passus I.–IV., I desisted, finding that it only tended to choke the foot-notes with inferior readings'[20]; and A had 'many corrupt readings'. Hence 'very little use has been made of this, as it seems an inferior MS.'; yet it 'furnished a few good readings at the end of Passus XI' (xxi–ii).

Of these seven MSS, the only ones that Skeat used to form his A Text, five (V, T, U and H^2) were already known to him when he put out his preliminary tract. In the intervening year before he published the A–Text, he did, evidently, consult the two MSS new to him, Douce 323 and Ashmole 1468, which indicates that he was certainly open to new ideas on the text.[21] Nevertheless, it is highly likely that Vernon's was the first A version of the poem that Skeat had read: and that inevitably, its text would tend to seem paradigmatic to him, with other versions to be compared against it – often skim-read against it – as a base, and rated as good or bad depending on their extent of agreement with Vernon.

All of this suggests that Skeat was pretty content with Vernon's text, and reluctant to rethink it substantially in the light of new evidence. Subsequent editors of A, who have had the benefit of Skeat's edition, and have been able to consult, on perhaps less prejudiced grounds, the MSS which he was crucially instrumental in bringing to light, have disagreed with him. Skeat himself came to accept many years later that he had been wrong to adopt Vernon as his base text. On 18 June 1909 he wrote to R.W. Chambers, his immediate successor in

19 See e.g. *North British Review*, o.s. 52 (n.s. 13), April 1870, 241, where Skeat's editing is described as 'almost faultless'.

20 1867, xxi.

21 The 1866 tract had, in fact, turned up a further three A–MSS, which Skeat describes in the same way as he has the previous ones, but which, as he explicitly says, he made no use of for his text. These were the imperfect copy in Lincoln's Inn, Harley 3954, and Digby 145.

editing A, to say 'My A–text was one of my earliest attempts: & I had no guide. The trouble was that no A–text had ever been printed. The B–text had been printed twice (Crowley & T. Wright): & the C–text by Whitaker. – I do not know whether you have ever tried editing a text from many MSS. for the first time. And then I did not know (no one knew) what MSS. existed! – Certainly, no one would now start with V as a basis. That was wrong. –'.[22]

Skeat was also, evidently, inclined to judge the worth of a MS on grounds which would not be wholly acceptable today: if there was a scribal overlay of corruption, as in the Lincoln's Inn MS, where the scribe seemed to have rewritten a number of lines in order to make them more alliterative, Skeat did not consider the possibility that it would be worthwhile collating the MS in full anyway, just in case the exemplar from which the Lincoln scribe (or whichever scribe in the history of transmission of the Lincoln MS) made his copy was actually a good and reliable version of the A–Text. This principle of course applies to *all* MSS, however corrupt they may seem – or as Skeat might have put it, with however many 'gross blunders' their text is defiled. Axiomatically, *all* versions of a text must descend from an authorial original, however far removed, which means that *some* original readings will have survived even in the most corrupt of texts. That this is so is shown by the fact that, by and large, MSS of the A–Text do present versions of the poem that are recognisably similar, or as George Kane put it in 1960, 'the majority of scribes did, after all, copy a very large number of words in a great many lines faithfully, often to the point of keeping spelling and dialect forms of the exemplar' (126). At some stage in its history, the Lincoln version may well have been a relatively good copy of the original text; hence one or two original readings might, in theory, have survived in places where all the other extant MSS have varying degrees of error.

It is clear, then, that Skeat's editing methods left much to be desired by later standards. He plumped for one MS as his base text on questionable grounds, and formed his views on other MSS on the basis of first impressions rather than rigorous and exhaustive examination of their respective texts. On the one hand, such an approach allowed him to put out his A–Text with astonishing speed; on the other, it caused problems for readers of the poem who took his A–Text to be an authoritative critical edition of A. (The principal victim here was Manly, as we shall see below.) It also began the process of setting in editorial stone the hypothesis that *Piers Plowman* existed in three versions and three versions only. What would have happened if Skeat had held his hand, spent several years reading as many MSS as he could get hold of, and turned up the version found in Bodley 851?

Skeat's edition of B, which followed two years later in 1869, used very similar methods. He relied mainly on MS Laud Misc. 581 as his copy-text, and collated

22 Chambers Papers item 5, University College London.

Rawlinson 38 (R, an interesting MS which Skeat regarded as representing an interim version between B and C), Trinity B 15 17 (the MS on which Wright's edition was based), and BL Add 10574 in full against it, incorporating their readings where he thought them superior to Laud's, and noting their readings in the critical apparatus if he thought them sufficiently interesting. Judging from his remarks about the other B–MSS known to him, he read these with variable care and attention. Thus he says of Corpus 201 (F), for example, that 'It is evidently an inferior MS.: yet it may be worth consulting in a case of difficulty', and he introduces some of its readings into his text (e.g. at XIV. 188), as well as recording the first and last lines of the MS's eccentric passus divisions. But he did not perceive the close relationship between F and R, despite the fact that these two MSS form one of the two separate branches of the B–MSS, and despite the fact that R was a MS which he had scrutinised very closely.[23]

There was an important development in his editorial practice between editing A and B, however. In both editions he gives a full description of each MS's appearance and contents, an indication of the probable date, and some characterization of the text to be found in each. But for the B–MSS he now provides an additional ingredient: a classification into sub-groups, although there is no discussion or illustration of the principles by which the sorting process has been conducted. This indicates some awareness of the 'scientific' school of editing now well established on the Continent, which followed Lachmann's recensionist principles: the idea being to establish the genetic relations between MSS by grouping them according to shared error.[24] However, Skeat's incomplete collation of the *Piers Plowman* MSS was not likely to produce a reliable result, and indeed his identification of sub-groups of MSS has not been supported by later editors.[25]

Skeat took much longer to edit C than he did the two previous texts. I suspect that this is because the MS tradition of C, like that of A, is complex. Skeat dispatched A very swiftly, probably because he did not fully grasp the problems it raised. B was also dealt with expeditiously, owing to the extraordinarily frequent unanimity of the MSS.[26] Skeat's description of the ups and

23 Skeat 1869, xxvii. The Athlone Press editors regard F as a significant witness to the B–Text and adopt many of its distinctive readings; see Kane and Donaldson 165–173.

24 Skeat 1869, xxx–xxxi. As is well known, English medieval editors lagged behind German and French editors in the textual sophistication with which they approached their MSS. See Sweet 10–16, and the implied criticism of Skeat's analysis of *Piers Plowman* MSS in his editions of A and B in Nichol 339–340.

25 See Kane and Donaldson 16–69.

26 Skeat's remarks on the textual consistency of the B–MSS are interesting in view of later editors' conviction that they present unprecedentedly knotty problems: '. . . there is a certainty, a firmness, and a conclusiveness about the text which is very satisfactory. There are probably more doubtful points in a single Canterbury Tale or in a single Act in some of Shakespeare's plays than in the whole of the B–text of Piers the Plowman. . . . I wish especially to draw the reader's attention to this, that he may remember, once for all, that any "conjectural emendations" are, in general, entirely out of the question' (Skeat 1869, xxxix).

downs he experienced in editing C give us some insight into the ways in which his editorial techniques had developed. He eventually took as his base text the same MS used by Whitaker, Hm 137. One would expect Skeat to have chosen a different MS, in order to increase the number of MSS in print and thus satisfy the good Furnivallian principle that was achieved by printing the Laud B–MS rather than Wright's Trinity MS. This was in fact his original view with the C–text: 'I thought it would be well to avoid printing the same one as had been printed already, because I considered that it would be a distinct gain to have two MSS. printed in full instead of one, and I rather disliked the look of Dr. Whitaker's text, as seeming to indicate a faulty source'. He chose instead the Cotton MS. Vespasian B. 16; 'but this plan soon broke down, as I found that it was constantly requiring emendation, or else that the readings were frequently inferior to those of Whitaker's edition'. He next tried the Earl of Ilchester's *Piers Plowman*, another good C version, 'but this MS. would not do to print from, on account of its incompleteness'. Finally he turned to the beautifully written Cambridge MS, FF. 5. 35, setting up the whole of its Passus II in type and collating the text with every other C–MS he knew of. 'Then the whole truth came out at last': that Whitaker's MS was in fact the best, but had been grossly disfigured in the printing. 'From this *corrected* copy of Whitaker', Skeat proudly announces, 'the present text has been printed, and the text is sufficiently satisfactory. Most of the absurd readings,' he continues,

> turned out to be Dr Whitaker's mistakes; some others were due to marked peculiarities in the scribe's spelling, easily removeable; and the rest have been amended by collation with six or seven other MSS. The resulting text is a peculiarly good one, and is, at any rate, ascertained on sufficient grounds to be the best that can be procured from the existing materials (1873, xxi–xxii).

This is an interesting account of his search for the right base–MS. Skeat's methods of editing have become vastly more sophisticated than they were in 1867, when he chose Vernon as a base–MS of A in a fashion that was not clearly argued or worked out. A sample collation of a significant stretch of the poem is an obvious way to embark on the struggle to rationalise and make some sense of a large number of different MSS. Presumably, also, Skeat had built up considerable expertise in recognizing typical patterns of scribal error, although he never discusses this point. Skeat continues,

> For a long time, the state of the text was a great puzzle to me, and it has been a great satisfaction to be able to find so full and clear a solution to that puzzle. I think it must have been nearly two years before I saw my way quite clearly; and I have no doubt that that chief part of the difficulty arose from my assuming that Dr Whitaker's print, so obviously *intended* to be correct, really *was* so. Certainly experience has taught me, as an editor, to put no trust in editors, but always to verify their work by a reference, where possible, to the originals which they profess to represent (xxii).

Experience has taught Skeat to be slower and more careful, and to test first impressions against a sufficiently large swathe of other evidence. His initial treatment of the C–MSS differs significantly from that of the A–MSS: *all* known MSS have been collated at least against Passus II, so as to get some idea of their general characteristics; and 'six or seven' additional MSS have been collated throughout rather than three (as with A and B). Subsequent editors, who have been able to learn both from Skeat's triumphs and his mistakes, have also heeded – in some cases – his advice to mistrust other editors, primarily, of course, Skeat himself. Consequently, they have taken considerably more time in completing and publishing their editions. Against any criticism of Skeat's swiftness and expedition, which at times seems to approach the slap-dash, must be weighed his extraordinary achievement of completing the three editions.

In order to assess his treatment of Z, it is illuminating to consider his treatment of another one of the C–MSS which gave Skeat much pause for thought, the Ilchester MS, of whose existence he had known from the beginning of his search for *Piers Plowman* versions. He collated this MS throughout, and commented, 'Perhaps no MS. could be better devised for completely puzzling a critic unfamiliar with the poem. The text has been made up from two imperfect texts, an A–text and a C–text; some of the matter comes twice over; several leaves have been lost; the remaining ones have been numbered wrongly, and then bound up in the wrong order. . . . The MS. has been somewhat spoilt, particularly at the end, by damp, and much injured by the rats, which have eaten away, in some places, nearly half the leaf, so that sometimes the last half, sometimes the first half of a line is entirely gone, and many lines are more or less imperfect' (xxxiii). Nevertheless, Ilchester was in many ways a remarkable MS. Its prologue, particularly, was notable for the insertion of lines that seemed to belong to much later in the poem, in Passus IX. Skeat's openmindedness to new information is illustrated by the fact that he does not dismiss these unconventional passages, but instead quotes from them with approval, commenting, 'These lines do not read to me as spurious; it is just possible that they represent the poet's first cast of this curious passage, peculiar as it is to the C–text' (xxxv). Skeat's conclusion on Ilchester is that it represents a separate branch of the C–text tradition. This has been confirmed by later scholars.[27] But his inference is a bold one:

> Just as MS. R [of the B–Text] differs from the true B–text in being of a somewhat later date and thus embodying a few after-thoughts, so MS. I differs from the true C–text, but in the other direction; for it is clearly an *earlier* draught of the C–text, and does not contain quite so many alterations of the text as do most of the other MSS. Its readings, in consequence, sometimes *point back* to the B–text (xxxvii).

Skeat struggled far more with the text of C than he had with his other editing

[27] Pearsall 1981, 181–93; Scase 1987, 456–63.

enterprises. Nevertheless, the extent of his knowledge of several of the MSS ran only to a comparison of their version of Passus II with the printed copy he had made up of F's text. His open-mindedness on Ilchester is remarkable, but perhaps explicable, like his attitude towards the Rawlinson B–MS, as the open-mindedness of someone still searching for a solution to an editorial problem, and not yet confident that he had found the answer.

Such, at least, is my explanation for why Skeat took such a different attitude towards the first of the two *Piers Plowman* versions preserved in Bodley 851 (which he suggested should be denoted by the letter Z, presumably because this was the last MS he came across). It is easy to reconstruct the manner in which Skeat finally discovered this MS, for he reports it himself with engaging candour (xxx–xxxiii):

> The copy of Piers the Plowman . . . was entirely unknown to me until quite recently. This oversight arose in the most natural way possible. When making my collection of "Parallel Extracts" [described above], Mr Coxe, Bodley's Librarian, whose kindness to me from first to last has been of the greatest service to me, himself sent me copies of the passage I had selected [near the start of Passus III] from the various MSS. of Piers the Plowman under his charge. But he sent me no copy from this MS. Z, for the sufficient reason that the passage is not to be found in it; whilst at the same time it never occurred to me to make further inquiry, because no other MS. omits this passage, and I did not suppose that any MS. *could* omit it. When however I at last lighted upon the MS. and examined it, this mystery was soon cleared up.

It turned out that Bodley 851 contained, like several other MSS, a hybrid text of the poem, made up of two separate components written in different hands:

> The first part exhibits an extremely corrupt text, mere rubbish, as it seems to me, and written out from imperfect recollection; but the latter part exhibits, though in a late hand, a copy of the C–text which is remarkable for the extreme general *correctness* of its readings, and may have been copied from an autograph or from an early copy of it.

Skeat observes, wrongly as it happens, that 'the former part of the MS. approaches rather to the B–text than the A–text . . . But the text is greatly corrupted, abridged, transposed, and in every way altered for the worse; so that it is worthy of no attention except as a curiosity'. To illustrate this, Skeat quotes from part of its description of the Deadly Sins (Z V 78–130; ff. 133^r–133^v), a passage abridged, he says, by cutting down B's 216 lines to 19, 'a considerable liberty'. The passage has several Norfolk allusions: Covetous's 'Norfolk' nose, his oath 'so thee ik', and the mention of the worsted that Covetous will give up making now that he is reformed.[28] (This local name for wool is derived from

28 The dialect form of Covetous's oath, found also in the B–Text (V 228) may well have been

the name of the town Worsted in Norfolk.) Curiously, instead of identifying the anti-Norfolk joke as a virtual commonplace in contemporary literature – found, among other places, in Chaucer's Reeve's Tale, and nearer still to home in Covetousness's B–Text protestation that he knows no French except that spoken in Norfolk[29] – Skeat rather jokily takes exception to the Z–poet's insults, and rises to Norfolk's defence. 'This description of Covetousness having "a Norfolk nose" contains some covert satire that is lost upon me. Having resided two years in Norfolk, I may be allowed perhaps to observe that I never remarked any peculiarity in the noses of the people there. But as they are, in these days at least, remarkably hospitable, this may account for my difficulty!!' And a propos the insinuation 'that the makers of the worsted fabrics at Worsted did not put in good work and workmanship', he comments, 'it is too bad to suppose that the convenient proximity of the shrine at Walsingham caused them to be careless of their commercial integrity'.

It is interesting, to say the least, that Skeat is content to write off, without further discussion, the distinctive characteristics of these lines as 'mere rubbish' (even though, in the case of Covetousness, they contain interesting expansions on the sin's characterisation in the other versions as a draper from Norfolk), while he was open to the possibilities presented by the unique lines, and unusual versions of orthodox lines, in Ilchester's and Rawlinson's texts. Z contains many other unique lines and readings, and several other unique passages, all of which, with one exception,[30] make satisfactory sense in context – or so it has been argued by Rigg and Brewer. When read through and considered on its own terms, it arguably produces a coherent and shaped narrative. But it seems unlikely that Skeat did read it through and consider it on its own terms. His remarks on the C portion of Bodley 851 indicate why this may have been so:

> . . . on comparing my printed C–text with the latter portion of [Z], I made the very satisfactory discovery that this MS., representing as it does a very pure text in spite of its rather late spellings, tended greatly to confirm the various emendations which I had made in the text after collation with other MSS. *It was, as it were, an unexpected and satisfactory testimony to the correctness of my text, confirming many results of careful thought, and shewing me that I had been working upon right principles* (my italics).

Skeat makes it clear that he came across Z right at the end of his editing process, after he had sorted out the puzzles and difficulties involved in teasing out from the MSS some sense of the probable authorial and transmission

the original reading of the A–Text as well; see the MS variants recorded by Kane 1960, at Passus V 142 (he does not consider the possibility in his discussion on 164).

29 B V 239; see Rigg and Brewer 16–17, 81.

30 The repetition of material between Passus IV and V; see Rigg and Brewer 14.

history of the poem.[31] The C portion of Z confirmed his theories, and was therefore highly acceptable to him – indeed he thought it possible the MS had been copied from the poet's autograph (xxiv n. 1) – while what he identified as the B portion of Z presented evidence that was simply indigestible in terms of his existing hypotheses, unless it was regarded as a scribal, not an authorial product. But those hypotheses had been formed on a preliminary view of the evidence. At the outset of the editing project, Skeat and Furnivall between them had set up a criterion for identifying a *Piers Plowman* MS, namely that it should contain certain lines from Passus III. Since Z did not satisfy this criterion, it was unidentified by the Bodley librarian, and slipped through their net. Skeat went on to establish and fix his ideas about the authorial process of composition of the poem, and its scribal transmission, without taking Z's eccentric version into account. When it surfaced several years later, he scanned the first section for recognisable passages, probably going first of all to the Deadly Sin episode because that was a swift and efficient way of working out which of the three versions Z most nearly corresponded to. What he found, as we saw, repelled him. His identification of the first part of Z as approaching 'rather to the B–text than the A–text' is illustrated by one line, also in Passus V, where Z does indeed agree with Skeat's edition of B rather than of A. But that is because Vernon reads uniquely at this point; most other A–MSS read the same as B – and as Z.[32] Skeat's A–Text reading for this line is an unfortunate consequence of his following the text of Vernon far too closely, without taking sufficient account of the other A–MSS. This oversight on Skeat's part seems to suggest that he glanced over the first part of Z, and rejected it almost immediately. His account of Bodley 851 effectively put it out of the running for serious consideration by later editors.

Skeat's pioneering work on *Piers Plowman* sorted out the plethora of MSS and versions into a clearly ordered structure; although, as we have seen, he established that structure in a somewhat haphazard way, making assumptions about the quality of the MSS and the way that the author had composed the poem without always rethinking these in the face of new evidence. In effect, he established three hypotheses on the poem, and these in turn determined the path that was to be taken by scholarly investigation of the work. The hypotheses were as follows: (i) that the poem originally existed in three and only three successively written versions, A, B and C (this notwithstanding Skeat's identification of at least two interim versions, as represented by the Rawlinson

31 A section of the type-set text of C Passus XVIII 1–20, scribbled over with corrections and addenda, survives in the Skeat-Furnivall collection at Kings' College London (F3a); 'Keep this: & note readings of Z' is written roughly across the top of the first page in what looks like Skeat's handwriting. Presumably this set of proofs was produced before Skeat had come across Z, but after he had established his text.

32 The MS variants are listed in the Athlone editions at A V 209 and B V 381; the corresponding lines in Skeat's texts are A V 218 and B V 388 respectively. Cf. Z V 106.

B–MS and the Ilchester C–MS); (ii) that his own editions of A, B and C presented a reasonably faithful picture of what Langland originally wrote; and (iii) that one author alone was responsible for the three original versions of the work. All three hypotheses were questionable. As it turned out, the last of the three was the first to be attacked. The next major development in *Piers Plowman* studies was the multiple-authorship theory put forward by J.M. Manly, the Chicago scholar and later editor of the *Canterbury Tales*, who in 1906 argued that the differences between A and B were such that B could not possibly have been written by the same person as A. In particular, he posited the existence of a 'lost leaf' in A, to explain certain characteristics of B, a version which he believed was written by a vastly inferior poet. Skeat's belief in single authorship was taken up and argued by R.W. Chambers, a lecturer at University College, London, who defended the third of Skeat's hypotheses by undermining the second. Chambers pointed out that Skeat's texts were not in fact 'critical' texts, i.e. put together with full consultation of all available manuscript evidence. Instead his A–Text, in particular, was based on Vernon, which Chambers demonstrated had in many cases unsatisfactory readings unlikely to represent the true and original A–Text. If one took instead the readings of (say) T, as representative of the A–Text, then many of the differences between A and B disappeared, and hence single authorship came to seem far less unlikely than Manly argued (Chambers and Grattan 1909). Manly eventually accepted that he had relied overmuch on Skeat's incomplete collations, and both sides acknowledged that Skeat's work needed to be done again.[33] But none of the contributors to either side of the *Piers Plowman* controversy, as it became known, questioned Skeat's first hypothesis, that Langland had written three and three only versions. Nor did they take up the suggestions that Skeat had at the same time, perhaps rather inconsistently, thrown out, that some MSS represented intermediate authorial stages between the three main versions.[34]

In about 1909, recognizing the provisional nature of Skeat's editions, Furnivall asked Chambers and his collaborator J.H.G. Grattan to prepare another edition of the A–Text for EETS, this time based on the Trinity A–MS, now generally acknowledged to be superior to Vernon, while one of Manly's Chicago graduate students, Thomas A. Knott, independently embarked on a rival edition of the same version in 1907. Chambers' edition never appeared, although he continued to work on it for the rest of his life. Knott's edition was eventually taken over by David C. Fowler, and was published under their joint names in 1952 after Knott's death. No mention of Bodley 851's *Piers Plowman*

33 Manly says as much in a letter to Chambers dated June 14, (?)1926: '. . . I did not realise how purely casual were Skeat's records of the readings [in the critical apparatus of his *Piers Plowman* editions] . . . Until we have a critical text of the three visions argument is futile'; Chambers Papers Item 41. The *Piers Plowman* controversy has been admirably summarised by Hussey (1952); see also Middleton 1986, 2224–27.

34 Cf. Donaldson 1955.

version is to be found in Knott-Fowler, not surprisingly given Skeat's failure to identify the first section of it as a version closer to A than to B or C. And no mention, similarly, is found in the papers relating to Chambers' projected edition of A preserved in his old College Library.

By the time he died, Chambers' *Piers Plowman* project had expanded into something far more ambitious than the original projected edition of A. Understanding, as had Skeat also, that it was impossible to establish the text of A without investigating the equivalent texts of B and C, he had set graduate students to work on the two latter versions. In 1940 he received a substantial grant from the Leverhulme Society to produce an edition of the three texts together; and it is evident that he was pursuing the project with far greater exhaustiveness and consistency than Skeat. After Chambers' death in 1942, the enterprise was inherited by Grattan, who swiftly enlisted the aid of the two most prominent of Chambers' graduate students: George Kane, a Canadian who had signed up for action almost immediately after his arrival at University College London, and A.G. Mitchell, an Australian who completed a PhD thesis on the C–Text under Chambers and who returned home shortly before the outbreak of war (Coffman 1945; Grattan 1951). After Grattan's death in 1951, Kane took over management of the entire project. He had inherited all Chambers' and Grattan's collations and papers on the A–Text, but decided to start again from scratch, transcribing the MSS anew and making up his own collations. He produced an edition of A in 1960. Again, this made no mention of the first *Piers Plowman* version to be found in Bodley 851. One possible reason for this is that Kane had departed from his predecessor's stated principle that, when preparing an edition of any one of the versions of the poem, the other version(s) should be consulted at the same time, since so much of the text of the two (or three) versions is in fact equivalent. Hence Kane had no reason to check through the MSS of the B and C versions, and hence no opportunity to discover that Skeat's description of Bodley 851 had been faulty.[35]

It is worthwhile reflecting on Kane's policy of confining himself to the evidence of the A–MSS when editing A. On the one hand, the policy's great advantage was that it limited the collation and editorial work to manageable dimensions, so that one person could take on and complete the edition within a reasonable space of time. The open-ended nature of Chambers' work on the poem, extending over many years, cannot have recommended itself as a desirable example to follow. On the other hand, the policy implies certain

35 See Chambers and Grattan 1916, 271: 'So inter-related are the texts, that before you can have a final A–text, you must have an adequate B– and C–text'; and Kane 1960 147 n. 1. Kane changed his mind on the necessity of consulting the other versions when he edited B; see Kane and Donaldson 75. I discuss some of the implications of this shift of policy in Brewer 1992.

assumptions about the versions of the poem, the author's composition of them, and their corruption through scribal transmission, none of which was clearly articulated or argued by Kane, but all of which can, with hindsight, be seen to have led him subsequently to reject Z as an authentic part of the *Piers Plowman* canon.

The reader of the poem desirous of making some sense of the textual and editorial history of the poem must ask the question whether these assumptions are valid. It is uncontroversial to claim that most of the 50-odd MSS of the poem fall into three different shapes, corresponding to what Skeat called A, B and C. But this implies a simpler set of relations between the three versions than in fact exists. Over significant stretches of the poem, all three texts read roughly the same, although the fifty-odd MSS vary in their exact rendering of these stretches. The patterning of variation does not necessarily correspond with the different versions; for example, some A–MSS may agree with B–MSS in one reading, whereas a rival reading may be found in other A–MSS and some C–MSS. (Since Kane did not consult other versions when editing A, he does not give any account of this complex set of relationships, which in many instances he seems to have been unaware of.) Under these conditions, how does an editor decide what is an A reading, a B reading, or a C reading? And how does an editor determine whether variation in readings in MSS of different versions over equivalent text is to be ascribed to authorial revision or faulty scribal transmission?

Standard criteria for distinguishing authorial from scribal readings – such as those enumerated by Kane in his edition of A – assume that the single 'best' reading among the variants ('best' on grounds such as sense, or poetic quality (however defined), or 'difficulty') will be the authorial one. Yet if one looks at variants drawn from three MS traditions, supposedly representing three single authorial versions, these criteria cannot necessarily apply. Will the difference between a good reading and a better reading be due to the fact that the good reading was the author's first version and the better his revision, or to the fact that the good reading was the scribe's corruption (for whatever reason) of the author's original? Many years ago, Kane's B–Text collaborator E.T. Donaldson noted the uncertainty of 'the assumption that a poetic revision will never produce the same mechanical pattern as a scribal error (Donaldson 1952–3, 271). Even more difficult is the question whether one might expect an author to improve his work as he revised it, or (in Whitaker's words) debase it. Certainly it is generally accepted that the poet's third version, C, is in some respects less poetically powerful than B; and one might therefore expect to find this where individual readings are concerned as well as in the case of lines and passages (which are made up of individual readings).[36]

All the above points are significant in assessing the origin and character of

[36] For a valuable critique of Kane's methods of editing, see Adams 1992. The present writer has also attempted some evaluation of Kane's work in Brewer 1989, 1991, and 1992.

the text found in Z. For example, many of the readings in Z are also found in B–MSS. If we accept the distinctions between the three versions established by Kane, we must suppose that the scribe of Z, although he predominantly followed an A–Text as his exemplar, periodically introduced B readings; the 'contaminated' quality of Z is one of the reasons Kane rejects this version as scribally corrupt. But most of the BZ readings are also found in other A–MSS as well, although not the A–MSS adopted by Kane as the basis of his edition of A. If Kane had been aware of Z from the outset, and had scrutinized the relations between the different versions line-by-line when establishing his A–Text, he might have come up with a different A– (and B–) Text, and might have regarded the many agreements between Z, A–MSS and B–MSS (and often C–MSS as well) as evidence for Z's authenticity.

Kane first mentions Z in a footnote to his edition of the B–Text, published in 1975 (14–15, n. 95). He had 'rightly dismissed [Z] as worthless for editorial use, but should have formally rejected [it] in Vol. 1', i.e. his 1960 edition of A. He judged it a 'conflated and sophisticated text', contaminated by both C and (to a less extent) B. Its A–Text was disordered, producing 'an imperfect or wholly inconsequent exposition', and omitting much authentic A–Text material. It also included 'many lines not relatable to any version, thus presumably spurious'. Some of the latter occurred 'at points of omission, as where the confessions of Envy and Avarice are reduced to thirteen lines of which ten are peculiar to Z'.[37] Kane put forward two suggestions for the existence of Z's curious version: 'One possibility is that the early part of Z was copied from a text produced by someone acquainted with all versions of the poem, literate and able to write tolerable long lines, who was restoring from memory, and occasionally by sophistication, a physically defective copy, very imperfect, or in many places defaced, or both, of the A version. The other possibility is that the whole of the 'A' component of the manuscript is merely a memorial reconstruction, the uneven quality of the text and the occasional coincidence of omission with sophistication being simply results of uneven recollection'.

This description stood until the publication of Rigg and Brewer in 1983. Their introduction took issue with many aspects of Kane's account of Z, claiming that the MS presented a coherent and self-sufficient version of the poem – albeit different from A, B and C. The quality of many of its unique lines and readings, together with the fact that several of the key episodes in the poem can be seen to be present in germ form in Z, led them to argue that Z represented a copy of an authorial version of the poem preceding the other three. They present their argument in full in their edition, examining the textual, literary,

[37] Kane also claimed that 'some of the groups of "new" lines occur where approximate multiples of 20 or 40 lines are wanting (i.e. the presumptive contents of sides or leaves)'; this argument has been authoritatively demolished by Green (1987).

linguistic and dating evidence and concluding that it is either neutral between the two explanations of Z's origin or points towards Z's authenticity.[38]

Rigg and Brewer's hypothesis has been variously received. Most notable was the review by George Kane published in *Speculum* in 1985, which condemned the edition without reserve. Other reviewers have been less harsh.[39] There has been a consensus that the date of the MS is difficult to fix with certainty, but also a recognition that the argument for Z's authenticity is not necessarily contingent on date. Several reviewers have agreed on the 'Langlandian' quality of some of Z's unique lines and passages, while acknowledging that judgement of such a quality must be subjective. Some have stressed the equivocal nature of the evidence, and the difficulty of deciding whether it supports an argument for scribal or for authorial origin.[40] Others have argued that the metrical patterns of Z's unique lines are otherwise found only in the A–, B– and C–Texts and hence are a strong indication that the same author was responsible for all four versions.[41]

It has also been recognized that the edition has damagingly undermined some of the implicit assumptions of the Athlone edition headed by George Kane, principally that the MSS represent three original versions of the poem and three only.[42] This assumption was vital to the Athlone project, for as one reviewer (Pearsall) pointed out, 'the practical necessities of the editor of a critical text' are such that he or she 'can have no truck with the idea of a continuously evolving text', such as implied by the existence of Z. The consequence of this assumption, in the opinion of another reviewer (Green), was that 'Kane and Donaldson have made Langland appear a neater and more consistent poet than even the most benevolent reading of his spiritual odyssey might lead one to expect'. If it is discarded, then readers' intuitions about Langland's writing habits may be better satisfied, but 'for future editors of his poem . . . the prospect it raises is truly daunting'.

The publication of the Z–Text and some of the interest it has excited are part of an increasing recognition of the importance of the scribe in Middle English writing. Over the last couple of decades, medieval textual critics have come to see the processes by which texts were transmitted and received as at least as proper a focus of attention as the words and/or intentions of the author, difficult (or impossible) as the latter are to recover. This shift in critical attention is, evidently, linked to a similar shift in critical theory as applied to

38 The present writer would now wish to correct the view expressed in Rigg and Brewer 22–25, that the textual evidence is neutral. She now believes it supports the case for Z's authenticity; see e.g. Brewer 1992.

39 See e.g. Pearsall 1985, Green 1984, Adams 1985, White 1984.

40 Cf. e.g. Pearsall's comment (1985, 182) that 'it has also to be acknowledged that every single argument in favour of the authority of Z as a pre–A version of the poem can be answered by arguments nearly as or equally good, or better, in favour of the traditional hypothesis'.

41 See Schmidt 1984, Duggan 1987. Another advocate of Z's authenticity (Allen, 1984) was persuaded by Langland's progressive use of the Psalter commentary of Hugh of St Cher.

42 See in particular Pearsall 181–2, and Green 131–2.

texts of a later period. The passion and intensity with which Kane pursues his search for Langland's *ipsissima verba* have been attributed by a number of critics to a romantic notion of the author as sublime, producing poetry of unique character and quality beyond the imitation of scribes (and incidentally, unlikely to be subject to authorial revision).[43] This view is regarded as anachronistic or irrelevant by a late-twentieth-century readership, which is likely to be more interested in the way the text was received by its contemporaries. And to many textual critics the ideal of recovering the author's original words will seem incapable of realisation, especially where *Piers Plowman* is concerned. Our access to authors and texts is controlled by scribes whose interests and aims in reproducing the text may have been quite different from ours.[44] Taken to its extreme point, this set of views tends to undermine Rigg and Brewer's claim for authenticity as much as it does Kane's Athlone edition, in that it renders the concept of authenticity irrelevant. If it is both impossible and uninteresting to recover an author's single original text – perhaps because such a thing never existed – then Z's worth is simply that of an available medieval text of the poem.[45]

This version of the poem is nevertheless a peculiarly fascinating one, given its significance in the history of the editing of *Piers Plowman*, and the unique quality and characteristics of its text. This is true whether one regards it as a copy of the author's first version, or as an example of scribal rewriting of a Middle English work. The publication of the MS of Z in facsimile form makes the primary evidence more readily accessible, and thus, it is hoped, contributes to the current debate on the proper way for a modern editor to present medieval texts to contemporary readers.

43 This observation has now become commonplace. See e.g. the important article by Lee Patterson (1987). On the matter of revision, see Shelley (1988) 294, col. 1.

44 Although only lately fashionable, this is an obvious point; cf. its characteristically commonsense expression in the following remarks by Skeat in a letter to R.W. Chambers dated 7 July 1909:

> There is a presumption that Wille was *himself* a scrivener: & one reason why he took so readily to rewriting things was precisely because he had no need to be beholden to any one for making his rough drafts. He could alter his work easily enough, because he *could do it himself*!
>
> Then his friends would borrow his rough-drafts which were . . . probably loosely (or well) bound. And his friends would copy them out (& a nice mess they sometimes made): & if any of them liked to add lines on his own account, there was nothing to prevent him. I believe we are utterly misled by modern notions, & clean forget how *casual* our ancestors were. How did *they* know that they were anything more than ephemeral productions? They looked upon them much more as we should regard a modern 'leading article'. They copied them because they wanted to *read them over again*! *not* because they wished to perpetuate them. They never regarded posterity one bit. What – as the famous remark runs – had posterity done for *them*?' (Chambers Papers Item 5.)

45 For further discussion of these points see Machan 1992, 15: 'the issue of who wrote the Z text may be far less important than that the Z text is; for the medieval reader who read it, the Z text was authorial – it was *Piers Plowman*'; and cf. Machan 1991.

MS Bodley 851

A. G. RIGG

Bodleian Library, Oxford, MS Bodley 851 (Bd) consists of three discrete parts.[1] The first part contains principally the unique text of Walter Map's *De Nugis Curialium*; the second is an anthology of miscellaneous Medieval Latin poems, mainly satirical; the third part contains *Piers Plowman*. Part I at least belonged to John Wells, monk of Ramsey, Oxford scholar, and prominent opponent of Wycliffe; as will be made clear below, it is probable that all three parts of the manuscript belonged to Wells. During the late fourteenth and fifteenth centuries more poems were added to the collection, and the three parts became a single volume. Textually, Part II has close affinities with Titus A. xx (Tx), Rawlinson B. 214 (Rb), Digby 166 (D), and Vespasian E. xii (Ve).

DESCRIPTION OF THE MANUSCRIPT[2]

209 leaves, including two end-leaves, numbered 1–210 (foliation skips 166). Parchment of uneven quality (a few holes or repairs). The binding, probably late medieval, consists of pasteboard with leather cover; the spine has been repaired in modern times; screwholes indicate the loss of two leather clasps.

Leaves measure approximately 235–245 × 175–180 mm. Writing area (excluding fly-leaves) Parts I–II 190 × 145 mm; III(a) 190 × 125; III(b) 185 × 125 mm. Parts I–II in two columns marked out in dry point or thin ink (prickmarks

1 This description was originally published as 'Medieval Latin Poetic Anthologies (II)', *Mediaeval Studies* 40 (1978), 387–407, and is reproduced with permission (Rigg 1978.) For the present purpose it has been revised in light of recent research, especially on bibliography, dating and localisation, and of course with reference to the Z-version of *Piers Plowman* (Rigg and Brewer 1983). The original article, however, is one of a series on poetic anthologies, and other articles in the series are relevant to the textual affiliations and origin of Bodley 851: namely, Rigg 1977, describing BL Cotton Titus A. xx (Tx) and Bodleian Rawlinson B. 214 (Rb), and Rigg 1979, describing Bodleian MSS Digby 166 (D), Bodley 603 (B), and BL Cotton Vespasian E. xii (Ve). Frequent reference is also made to my *A Glastonbury Miscellany of the fifteenth Century* (Oxford, 1968), which describes Cambridge, Trinity College, MS 0.9.38 (Ty).

2 For older descriptions of the manuscript, see Madan and Craster, 1922, No. 3041, and R.L. Poole and M.R. James in James' edition (1914) of the *De Nugis Curialium*, cited below on No. 1 (p. 33).

visible for verticals), horizontal lines in dry point (prickmarks visible only in quire ix, fols 82–89); Part III(a) long lines, frames and ruled in dry point; Part III(b) long lines, framed only.

Decoration: Parts I–II have inset display initials (2–3 lines deep) in blue, with red interiors and scrollwork; alternating red and blue paragraph marks (for which guide marks are still visible); red and blue initials for stanzas (No. 18); occasional red initials (Nos 9–14); red touching to initials (Nos 7 and 9); book and chapter headings, and running heads (No. 1), in red. Part III(a) has inset initials (blue with red work) for Passus I–VIII. Part III(b) is decorated in a different style, with red-touched initials and red underlining only (and a solitary deep blue initial on fol. 150r). In the upper part of fol. 6v is an elaborate book-plate: the name WELLIS is written in large scrolls; a bear on the left side pulls with his chain at the bow of the W; on the right side St Christopher carries the Christ-child, and his staff pierces the S. Extensions of the ascenders of the W contain the words 'Iste liber constat Fratri Iohanni de' and those of the LL have 'Monacho Rameseye'.[3]

Collation of leaves: earlier divisions[4]

Fly-leaves: fols 1–6
i^4 ii^2 (inner bifolium excised, with loss of text): fol. 6v numbered 'j' in the final quiring.

Part I: fols 7–77
iii^{12} (fols 7–17, lacks leaf after fol. 7, with loss of text), iv^{12}–viii^{12} (fols 18–77). Catchwords on fols 17v, 29v, 41v, 53v, 65v. Fols 74ra–77v originally blank; fol. 77v extremely worn.

Part II: fols 78–123
*ix missing, with loss of text (lost after final quire numbering), ix^{12}–xi^{12} (fols 78–113), xii^{10} (fols 114–123). Catchwords on fols 89v, 101v, 113v. Earlier quire number 'iii' on fol. 90r (the beginning of the original third quire, before the loss of quire *ix). Fols 120vb–123v originally blank; fol. 123v worn.

Part III(a): fols 124–139
xiii^8–xiv^8. Early quiring marks fols 132–135 'b', 'b ij', 'b iij' and 'b iiij' on the recto side. The first scribe ended his writing on fol. 139r.

3 For a fuller description, see James (1914), and facsimile, fol. 6v.

4 In the final series of quire numbers (from what is now quire ii to xxiii) the numbers are on the last verso side; these must be distinguished from earlier series, which are on the recto sides at the beginning of the quires.

Part III(b): fols 140–208

xv^{6}–xvii^{6} (fols 140–157), xviii^{8} (fols 158–165), xix^{10} (fols 167–176: the paginator has skipped 166), xx^{8}–xxiii^{8} (fols 177–208). An early quiring marks fol. 140r 'j', fol. 146r 'ij', and so on, up to quire xxiii; the first four leaves of each quire are lettered a–d, from which it can be seen that the outer bifolium of quire xvi was lost *before* writing (fol. 146r is 'ij b', etc.), and that fols 203–206 have been disordered *since* writing (correct order: 204, 203, 206, 205). As noted above, the decoration of Part III(b) differs from that of Parts I–III(a).

Scribes[5]

B wrote fols 78ra–81va (and presumably the missing quire *ix), Nos. 6–7 at the beginning of Part II. Anglicana Formata; 47 lines per column.

C re-ruled fols 82–89 and wrote the beginning of No. 9 on fols 81vb–83va; Anglicana Formata; 48 lines per column.

A wrote most of Part I, Nos. 1–2 on fols 7ra–73vb; his Anglicana Formata script becomes distinctly more sloping after fol. 30r; 42 lines per column. On fol. 33ra he left a gap of 15 lines, which he later filled, using a more cramped style of writing. He continued to write in Part II, from fol. 83va–115vb, writing 41 lines per column (ignoring the ruling by C), concluding No. 9 and then writing Nos. 10–14.

X wrote No. 3 on fols 74ra–74va (49 lines per column), No. 8 on fol. 81va and No. 18 on fols 118va–120vb (48 lines per column); in collaboration with S he wrote Nos. 15–17 on fols 116ra–118rb (here *X* writes 50 lines per column, S 54). *X* also wrote Part III(a), fols 124r–139r, using a darker ink (50 lines per page). He was responsible for the rubric headings in Parts I and II and in the bookplate on fol. 6v. He wrote a small neat Anglicana Formata script, with some broken strokes; hand S is an even smaller version of the same script.

A scribe called Dodsthorp wrote most of the entries on fols 2r and 3r, the *Miles Gloriosus* on fol. 5r–v (2 columns, 54 lines), No. 5 on fols 75va–76rb (using the original layout, 45–47 lines per column), and No. 20 on fols 120vb–123ra (at first re-ruling for 43 lines, then increasing to as many as 58). He has two scripts, one somewhat more formal than the other with some Secretary features.

Hand *Y* wrote No. 4 on fols 74va–75rb, 76va (a sloppy Anglicana hand).

Hand *Q* wrote the rest of *Piers Plowman* in Part III(b) on fols 139r–208r: he marked out a frame but did not rule lines (he varies between 29–36 per page).

As noted above, the inscription in the bookplate on fol. 6v by hand *X* reads: 'Iste liber constat Fratri Iohanni de WELLIS Monacho Rameseye'. Does this refer to Part I alone, to Parts I and II, to Parts I, II, and III(a), or to any other single section? This question (which cannot finally be answered) can best be

5 On the order in which these scribes wrote, see the following section.

seen in perspective after an analysis of the procedure of compilation. Evidence for this comes from the sequence of writing and the stages of decoration.[6]

(1) Part II (up to fol. 83va, including the now missing quire *ix) was written by hands *B* and *C*; part of fol. 81va was left blank.
(2) Part I (fols 7ra–73vb) was written by hand *A*, who also took over Part II and completed it to fol. 115vb. The following leaves were still blank: fols 74r–77v, 81va, and 116ra–123v.
(3) Hand *X* now filled the blank column fol. 81va with No. 8, and wrote No. 18 on fols 118va–120vb. This left the following blank: fols 74r–77v, 116ra–118rb, and 120vb–123v.
(4) Hand *X* supplied rubric headings in Parts I and II, and the inscription on fol. 6v (thus adding what was originally a four-leaf quire, now fols 5–6).
(5) Hand *X* also wrote Part III(a): using two quires of eights he wrote out *Piers Plowman* A–text up to VIII. 88, what we believe is to be called the Z–version. He stopped near the foot of fol. 139r, leaving a few lines and fol. 139v blank.
(6) Up to this point all written texts had been prepared for decoration, either by leaving gaps (with cue letters) for initials or by providing marginal indicators for paragraph marks. This decoration was now supplied in all sections, including Part III(a).[7]
(7) Hand *X* contined to fill the manuscript, writing No. 3 on fol. 74ra–va, No. 19 on fol. 120vb, and, in collaboration with *S*, wrote Nos. 15–17 into fols 116ra–118rb (most of column 115vb was left blank). No space was provided, nor indication given, for the decoration of these items. This still left some leaves blank in both Parts I and II.

John Wells's 'Book', therefore, could refer to any of these stages in the manuscript's history. The *liber* of the bookplate might refer simply to the *De nugis curialium* (cf. the heading on fol. 7r 'In libro magistri Gauteri Mahap'), and hence only to Part I. General uniformity of appearance, however, suggests that Parts I and II could be regarded as a unit (i.e. after decoration, but excluding Part III(a)). Thirdly, as hand *X* was also responsible for writing Part III(a), and as this part was included in the decoration, one could regard the book as containing all parts completed by the end of stage (6) or (7).

Later additions

(8) Some time in the fifteenth century, the apparently deficient *Piers Plowman* was finished by hand *Q*. He took an already prepared booklet of nine

6 The sequence is illustrated on the accompanying chart.

7 Some decoration is missing at the beginning of No. 9: the second column has red and blue paragraph marks; in the first column the title is underlined in red, and initials are touched in red, but marginal indicators are provided at lines 31 and 43. Gaps at the beginning of lines 17–18 may be for missing words (*Mox* and *Criso-*) but there is also a paragraph indicator beside 17.

quires (xv–xxiii), numbered and lettered (with the outer bifolium of quire xvi already missing). He first used the end of the original Part III(a), and finished the A–text to the end of Passus VIII on fol. 140v (= Q^1); he then continued on fol. 141r with C–text Passus XI to the end of the poem (= Q^2). This part was then decorated in a different style. For the nature of Q^1 and Q^2, see Rigg-Brewer, especially pp. 28–30.

(9) The whole manuscript, from quire ii to xxiii, was provided with a new set of quire numbers. An extra set of fly-leaves, fols 1–4, was added; most of fol. 2v had already been filled. A scribe named Dodsthorp filled fols 2r and 3r, wrote the *Miles Gloriosus* on fols 5r to the middle of the gathering, No. 5 on fols 75va–76rb, and No. 20 on fols 120vb–123ra. Dodsthorp still planned some decoration: he left a gap for a rubric title on fol. 5ra (and perhaps some signs for paragraph marks), paragraph signs in No. 5, and gaps for rubric initials in No. 20. This decoration, however, was never supplied. Dodsthorp's name does not appear in the list of monks present at the visitation of the bishop of Alnwick in 1439: the entries, therefore, must be dated later than 1439, unless he was away from Ramsey at the time.[8] At about this time fol. 208v was filled.

(10) Hand Y wrote No. 4 on fols 74va–75rb, and then, finding fols 75va–76rb occupied, noted 'require in secundo folio post' and completed the text on fol. 76va. Unfortunately, No. 5 was still unfinished (after three lines of a stanza). Dodsthorp, however, supplied a colophon to No. 4 and filled in a missing line.[9]

(11) The writing was now complete. Extra end-leaves (fols 209–210) were added, and the whole manuscript was bound: the front pastedown is from some abbey accounts, the end pastedown from the legal text which supplied fols 209–210. Some time before foliation a leaf was lost before fol. 8, and a quire was lost before fol. 78, and leaves 203–206 were disordered. The foliation was completed to 208 (fols 209–210 are numbered in a modern hand).

Fly-leaves and pastedowns

The pastedown on the front cover contains accounts (s. xv) relating to Ramsey; that on the back cover, and the two preceding leaves (fols 209–210,

8 I am grateful to Professors Edwin DeWindt and Ambrose Raftis for information on Ramsey names: an Alice Dodsthorp is recorded in the village in the early fifteenth century. Dodsthorp's mannered hand (with an elaborate *þ* and short *r*) can be seen on the fly-leaves, on fol. 5r lines 1–9, fol. 120vb lines 1–12 and titles, and fol. 75vb stanzas 1–2 and from halfway down fol. 76rb. His other style is Anglicana.

9 This cumbersome procedure (which assumes that Y and Dodsthorp were writing at the same time) is necessary to explain the unfinished state of No. 5, the break in No. 4 from fol. 75rb to 76va, and Dodsthorp's colophon to No. 4.

are from a legal treatise in an early fourteenth-century hand. Fols 1–4, perhaps added by Dodsthorp himself, form a separate set of fly-leaves, not included in the final series of quire numbers; they now contain:

(i) fol. 1r: old Bodleian shelf marks;[10]
(ii) fol. 1v: two inscriptions (s. xvi/xvii):
 (a) Saepe sub incultis reperitur gemma lapillis
  Saepe cadus vilis nobile nectar habet.[11]
 (b) In remotissima posteritate mihi faciet authoritatem antiquitas, quia tunc, ut nunc, vetustum cuprum praeferetur auro novello, etc. in eam sententiam.[12]
(iii) fols 2r–3r: proverbs and short poems (see Appendix);
(iv) fols 3v–4r blank;
(v) fol. 4v: two short poems (Appendix 76–77) and (s. xv) a table of consanguinity.

Textual relationships

The textual relationships of an anthology or of a composite manuscript (and Bd is both of these) consist not only in the relationship of individual texts but also of the collection as a whole. A group of manuscripts of the twelfth to the fifteenth centuries – Tx, Rb, Bd, Ve, D, B, and Ty – share many common items but are not necessarily always in the same textual families; these manuscripts are discussed in the articles and book cited in no. 1 above; for a chart of common elements, see 'Medieval Latin poetic anthologies (III)', pp. 502–3. A manuscript in this group may owe its text of one item to one manuscript, and of another item to another manuscript. A close textual relationship (for example, showing common errors) implies a real copying; when such a relationship is shared among different members of the group, we are dealing with an interchange of texts – not the direct copying of whole manuscripts but of elements of each. The only circumstances in which this can arise is where several manuscripts were available for selection and copying: for example, between nearby or affiliated monasteries, or in a university.

Bd is almost certainly related to the ancestor of the sister-manuscripts Tx and Rb: with both it shares Nos 7, 15, 16, and 18; with Tx it shares Nos 5, 9, 13, 14 and 20; with Rb it shares flyleaf poem No. 43. Both Bd and Tx have

10 A list is provided in Poole's description (James's edition, p. vii), but the order of entries is cancelled in the *corrigenda* sheet.

11 Walther *Sprichwörter* 27317, from here only; the verses were probably written after the following quotation. As noted below, the hand is not identifiable.

12 The quotation is from the end of Distinctio IV of the *De nugis*; the words are underlined in the text, fol. 47rb.

poems by Walter of Wimborne (Bd No. 6, Tx No. 67); with the anti-Norfolk jibe in fly-leaf No. 49 compare TxRb's poem against Norfolk (Tx No. 64). Tx's short version of No. 5 (*Convocacio sacerdotum*) could be derived from the immediate ancestor of Bd. On the other hand, Bd's version of No. 14 (*Speculum Stultorum*) is in a separate textual family from Tx; this may be true also of No. 13 (*Babio*).

In No. 7 (*De coniuge non ducenda*) Bd is very closely related to Ve and Ty (of which Ve certainly, and Ty probably, were compiled in Oxford); the group BdVeTy, in turn, is closely related to TxRb. With the Bekynton Anthology (Bodleian, Add. A. 44), these manuscripts form a closely knit family.

In addition to No. 7, Bd shares Nos 2, 14, and 18 with Ve; No. 2 is unique to the two manuscripts. In No. 18 Bd is in a separate textual family from Ve.

There are also striking similarities in content between Bd and Bodleian MS Digby 166 (ss. xiv, xv = D): they share Nos. 7, 8, 10–11, and 18; No. 3 is an extract from a text which is complete in D. Both D and Rb share poems by Walter of Peterborough (see Rb No. 27); D's 'Prisciani regula' is a separate version of Bd's No. 5. In No. 7 D's text is in a quite separate tradition, and in Nos. 10–11 D is in the *mu* group, quite separate from Bd. It is, in fact, quite common to find anthologies which share many poems, but which are not always textually related: in these cases we are dealing with literary relationships and suggestibility. That is, a compiler would derive his idea for his contents list (his 'model') from a similar manuscript, but might choose to copy his text from elsewhere.

Provenance

The Ramsey associations of the manuscript are clear, in the entries on the front pastedown and on fol. 208v and in the bookplate on fol. 6v. Some of the short poems on the front fly-leaves also show local interest (e.g. No. 3 on Wells). There is no objection to identifying the John Wells of the bookplate with the 'rather famous' anti-Wycliffite.[13] He was a scholar of Gloucester College, Oxford, before 1376, and *prior studentium* (1381); he was a prominent figure at the council at Black Friars in 1382, and was appointed proctor on behalf of the provincial chapter of English Black Monks to go to Rome to plead for the release of Cardinal Adam Easton; he died in Perugia in 1388.

On the other hand, there is evidence that the book itself was compiled in Oxford. First, the bookplate implies that the book was not always at Ramsey: otherwise, why identify it as the property of a Ramsey monk? Second, the textual affiliations just discussed with Ve and Ty in No. 7 (and similarities to D) can best be explained by Bd's participation in an Oxford 'pool' of poetic

[13] For biographies of Wells, see James's edition, the article by T.F. Tout in the *Dictionary of National Biography*, and Emden 1957–59, and articles cited there.

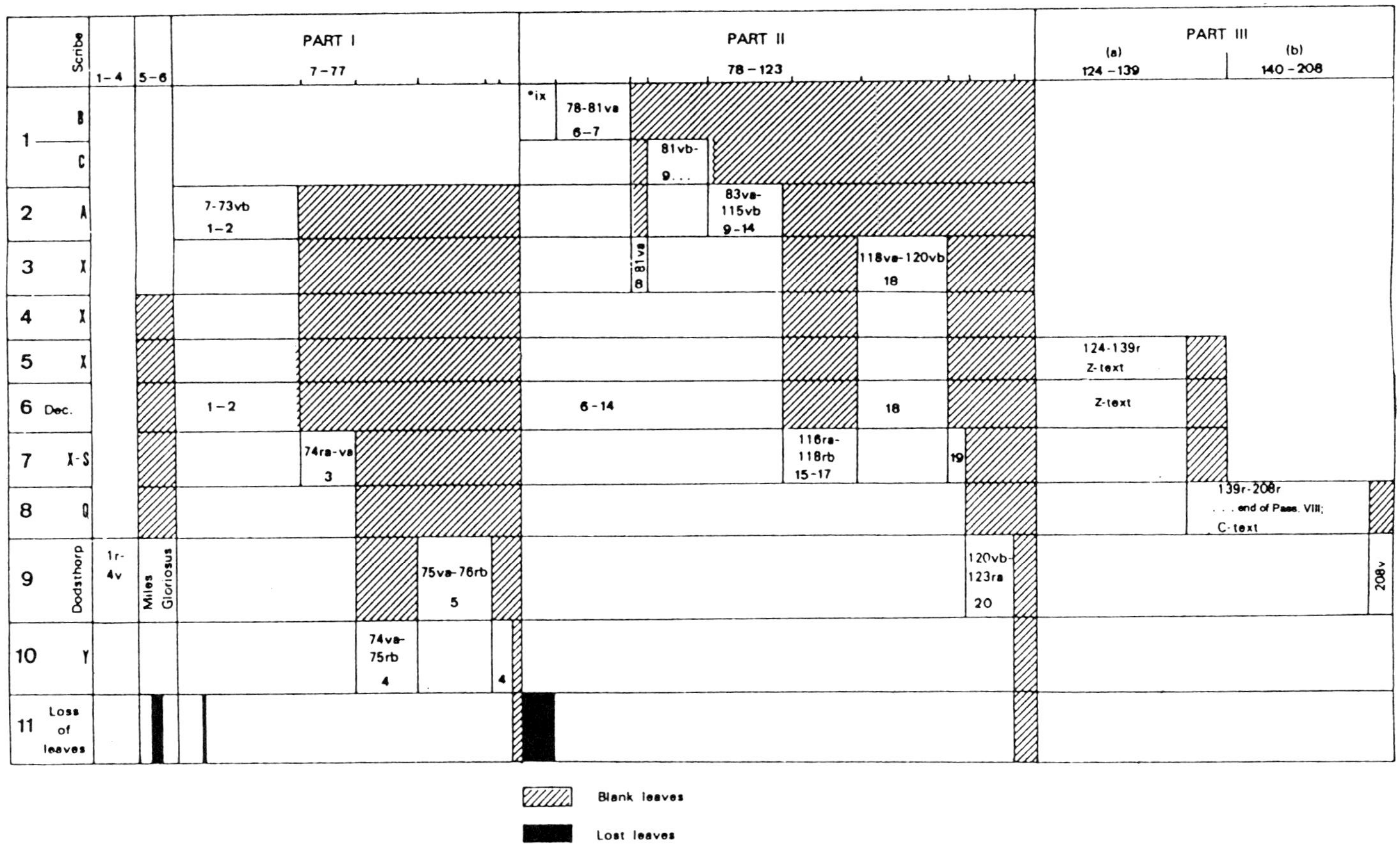

Scribe
1–4
5–6
PART I
7–77
PART II
78–123
PART III
(a)
124–139
(b)
140–208
1 B
C
2 A
3 X
4 X
5 X
6 Dec.
7 X-S
8 Q
9 Dodsthorp
10 Y
11 Loss of leaves
*ix
78-81va
6–7
81vb-
9...
7-73vb
1–2
83va-
115vb
9–14
81va
8
118va-120vb
18
124-139r
Z-text
1–2
6-14
18
Z-text
74ra-va
3
116ra-
118rb
15-17
19
139r-208r
... end of Pass. VIII;
C-text
1r-
4v
Miles
Gloriosus
75va-76rb
5
120vb-
123ra
20
208v
74va-
75rb
4
4
Blank leaves
Lost leaves

anthologies. (Connections with TxRb, both closely associated with monastic houses, could also point to a university origin: the compilers of Tx and Rb could well have attended university at some time). Third, No. 1, a copy of Map's *De Nugis Curialium*, could derive from an original preserved in Oxford from the time when Map was archdeacon (1197).

The accounts on the flyleaves suggest that the manuscript returned to Ramsey, but it is also possible that Dodsthorp was in Oxford when the later additions were made.

Date

The *terminus ad quem* for stages 1–7 of the compilation is the death of Wells in 1388. The *terminus a quo* is 1350, the probable date of No. 12, John of Bridlington's *Prophecy* (see below, p. 36); the compilation certainly dates from after 1346, when Nos. 15–16 were added. The most probable date is the early 1370s, when Wells was a scholar at Gloucester College.

The date of Dodsthorp's additions is less certain. Although his name is not on the list of monks present at the visitation of 1439 (see p. 27), he may have been away from Ramsey at the time. The only firm date is 1405, the death of Archbishop Scrope (no. 4, by hand Y).

The contents

It is an interesting collection for an anti-Wycliffite to own, if the bookplate refers to more than just Part I. Satirical writings predominate – Walter Map's *De nugis curialium*, the *Speculum stultorum* and *Apocalypsis Goliae*, the political satire of John of Bridlington's *Prophecy*, the antifeminist *De coniuge non ducenda* – as well as other kinds of poems, devotional (Wimborne's *Ave virgo*), moral (debate between Heart and Eye), historical (Troy poems), dramatic (*Babio*), and 'virtuoso' (the poetic debate between Michael of Cornwall and Henry of Avranches). Quite probably the Z–text of *Piers Plowman* was also attached to the collection when Wells owned it. Later additions, after stage 7, emphasize the heterogeneity: X added the political poems Nos. 15–16 and the anti-friar section of Satan's Epistle, and much later Dodsthorp added two plays and the satire on clerical celibacy, as well as the equally heterogeneous collection of epigrams and verses on the fly-leaves; Y added another poem of historical interest (No. 4).

Recent history and annotations

Explanatory notes and variant readings have been provided for the *De nugis* by a near-contemporary hand; another note on fol. 90v may be by hand A. Occasional marginal stalked flowers may be by Dodsthorp, who draws flowers beside his fly-leaf entries. Experimental scrollwriting can be seen on fols 18r, 162r, 193r, 194r, and 200r. On fol. 208v is pencilled the name 'J. Kyngston' (s. xv); the same hand has written notes on fol. 207v (pencil) and possibly fols 159r, 172v, 195v and 197v. On fol. 208v, in ink, is the date 'Anno domini millesimo quingentesimo quinto'. On fol. 6v is the name 'Whyttynton' (s. xv).[14] Slightly later hands have supplied notes on the date of the *De nugis* (fol. 7r) and the authorship of John of Bridlington's *Prophecy* (fol. 90rb).

The two inscriptions on fol. 1v have already been mentioned; the second is by a hand which also made frequent notes throughout the text of the *De nugis* (fols 20r, 20v, etc.): it is not that of any of the more obvious antiquaries, such as Thomas Bodley, William Camden, Brian Twyne, Thomas or Richard James, Bishop Ussher, or Thomas Hearne. It may be that of Cuthbert Ridley, who presented the book to the Bodleian Library in 1601: Ridley came from Northumberland, matriculated 1593, B.A. 1596, M.A. 1599, was licenced to preach 1604, rector of Simondsburn, Northumberland, 1604.[15] As noted above, fol. 1r bears several old Bodleian shelf marks.

CONTENTS[16]

Fly-leaves: fols 5–6[17]

Miles Gloriosus

fol. 5ra Vernat eques iam prima genis lanugo susurrat
fol. 5vb . . . *ends incomplete at line 204*

Walther 20216. Ed. Silvano Pareto, in *Commedie latine del XII e XIII secolo* IV (Genoa, 1983), pp. 11–93. Bd, like two other manuscripts, omits lines 1–2. The inner bifolium has been cut out: the remaining 162 lines would have occupied just over three columns. Scribe: Dodsthorp (cf. Nos. 5 and 20 below).

14 The *Summary Catalogue* also records the name 'Th. Strype' on fol. 2 (s.xvi), but this is no longer legible.

15 J. Foster, *Alumni Oxonienses 1500–1714* 3 (Oxford, 1891), p. 1257; Ridley also presented MSS. Bodley 94, 365, and 603, but his hand is not to be seen there.

16 In this account of the contents, reference is made, by number, to Hans Walther, *Initia carminum ac versuum medii aevi posterioris latinorum*, 2nd ed. (Göttingen, 1969), and to his *Proverbia sententiaeque latinitatis medii aevi*, 5 vols (Göttingen, 1963–67), cited as *Sprichwörter*. Reference is also made, by short title, to T. Wright, *Poems commonly attributed to Walter Mapes*, Camden Soc. (London, 1841), and his *Political poems and songs relating to English history from the accession of Edward III to that of Richard II*, 2 vols, Rolls Ser. (London, 1858–61).

17 For the contents of fols 2r–4v, see Appendix below.

Part I: fols 7–77

1. Walter Map: De nugis curialium

fol. 7ra IN LIBRO MAGISTRI GAUTERI MAHAP DE NUGIS CURIALIUM. DISTINCTIO PRIMA. ASSIMULACIO CURIE REGIS AD INFERNUM. CAPITULUM PRIMUM

In tempore sum et de tempore loquor . . .

fol. 72vb *List of contents by chapter*

fol. 73va EXPLICIT DISTINCTIO QUINTA LIBRI MAGISTRI GAUTERI MAHAP DE NUGIS CURIALIUM

Ed. M.R. James, C.N.L. Brooke and R.A.B. Mynors (Oxford, 1983). I sometimes refer to the older edition by James (Anecdota Oxoniensia, Med. and Mod. Ser. 14; Oxford, 1914) with its additional information by R.L. Poole. Bd is the sole manuscript, except for the antimatrimonial section, *Epistola Valerii ad Ruffinum philosophum*, which was very popular and the subject of many learned commentaries. Near-contemporary annotations, especially in Dist. 4, show knowledge of another manuscript; James says that the hand is X, but this is uncertain.

2. Fall of Carthage

fol. 73va CAUSA EXCIDII CARTAGINENCIUM

Narrat flaccensius in hystoriis . . .

fol. 73vb . . . vt patet superius per ordinem

Ed. James (1914) (see No. 1), pp. 260–61 (and p. 271). Another text, with only slight differences, is in London, British Library MS. Cotton Vespasian E. xii.

3. Epistola Sathanae

fol. 74ra Porro sobrios viros . . .

fol. 74va . . . vmbra pretereunt non attendant

This is a short extract from the 'Epistola Sathane ad vniversalem ecclesiam' (*inc.* Princeps regionis iehennalis), ed. W. Wattenbach, 'Über erfundene Briefe in Handschriften des Mittelalters, besonders Teufelsbriefe', *Sitzungsberichte der königlich preussischen Akademie der Wissenschaften zu Berlin*, Jahrgang 1892, Erster Band, pp. 91–123 (text pp. 104–16). Wattenbach edits from Reims, Bibliothèque Municipale MS. 1275 (olim 743; s. xiii, last quarter), recording also Digby 166 and Vienna, Österreichische Nationalbibliothek MS. Theol lat. 110 (s. xvi); it is also in London, British Library MS. Harley 913. The extract in Bd deals satirically with the Franciscans.

4. Execution of Archbishop Scrope (1405)

fol. 74va Quis meo capiti dabit effundere

fol. 76va . . . Vt spretis infimis letemur superis

Explicit processus martirii Ricardi Scroup Eboracensis archiepiscopi

Walther 16078. Ed. Wright, *Political Poems* 2. 114–18, from London, British Library MS. Cotton Faustina B. ix only: the Bd version differs in minor details, and has two extra stanzas on the archbishop's companion (after stanza 3 on p. 116) and six extra stanzas (after the first stanza on p. 118) showing extreme bitterness towards the king and the state of the kingdom. Text by hand Y: it breaks off at the foot of fol. 75rb (with a note by Y 'require in secundo folio post') and ends on fol. 76va.

5. **Convocacio sacerdotum**

fol. 75va Examinacio sacerdotum propter concubinas
Nouus rumor anglie partes pergirauit
fol. 76rb . . . Et qui prius fuerant artibus inbuti

Walther 12337. Ed. Wright, *Mapes*, pp. 180–82, from Tx and London, British Library MS. Cotton Vitellius A. x: see Tx No. 63. Bd's version of 45 stanzas (unedited) is quite the longest, but is deficient, ending with the third line of a quatrain at the foot of the page. Evidently Y entered No. 4 before Dodsthorp (this scribe) had finished; Dodsthorp, however, supplied the colophon to No. 4.

Remainder of fol. 76v and all fols 77r–77v blank. Fol. 77v very rubbed.

Part II: fols 78–123

6. **Walter of Wimborne: Ave virgo**

fol. 78ra Venus urit lubrica
fol. 80rb . . . Dapibus ambrosiis

Ed. A.G. Rigg, *The Poems of Walter of Wimborne*, O.F.M. (Studies and Texts 42; Toronto, 1978), pp. 111–83. This is part of the A–text, beginning at 88/6; the complete text is in Corpus Christi College, Oxford MS. 232 (c. 1300), where it is preceded by the *De mundi vanitate*. The missing quire *ix in Bd (assuming that it consisted of twelve leaves) could have contained at least these two poems.

7. **De coniuge non ducenda**

fol. 80va Sit deo gloria laus benediccio
fol. 81va . . . Nec dolor coniugis habet remedium. Explicit

Walther 18302. Ed. A.G. Rigg, *Gawain on marriage: the textual tradition of the 'De coniuge non ducenda' with critical edition and translation* (Studies and Texts, 79; Toronto, 1986), with full account of the textual affiliations of Bd.

8. **Philip the Chancellor: Debate between Heart and Eye**

fol. 81va Si quis cordis et oculi non sentit in se iurgia
fol. 81va . . . Nam cordi causam imputat occasionem oculo

Walther 17915. Ed. Wright, *Mapes*, pp. 93–95; B. Hauréau, *Notices et extraits de quelques manuscrits latins de la bibliothèque nationale*, 1 (Paris, 1890), pp. 365–7 (from Paris, B.N. MSS lat. 8433, 3718, 11867, 456, nouv. acq. lat. 1544). See H. Walther, *Das Streitgedicht in der lateinischen Literatur des Mittelalters*, 2nd ed., ed. P.G. Schmidt (Hildesheim, 1984), pp. 62–63. Bd uses a long-line format, producing seven quatrains; the variants correspond fairly closely to those of Cambridge University Library Dd. 11. 78 and the Camden text, as reported by Wright.

9. **Debate between Michael of Cornwall and Henry of Avranches**

fol. 81vb VERSUS MAGISTRI MICHAELIS CORNUBIENSIS CONTRA MAGISTRUM HENRICUM ABRINCENSEM CORAM DOMINO HUGONE ABBATE WESTMONASTERII ET ALIIS
Archipoeta vide quod non sit cura tibi de
fol. 83va CORAM MAGISTRO H. DE MORTUO MARI OFFICIALI CANTUARIENSIS ARCHIEPISCOPI
Quid me sollicitas qua sollicitudine citas
fol. 85rb CORAM DOMINO ELECTO WINTONIENSI ET EPISCOPO ROFENSI
Pendo poeta prius te diximus archipoeta
fol. 89ra . . . An sis conductus ductus fur ad fora luctus

Walther 1432. Ed. A. Hilka, 'Eine mittellateinische Dichterfehde', in *Mittelalterliche Handschriften. Festgabe zum 60. Geburtstage von Hermann Degering* (Leipzig, 1926), pp. 123–54, from all five manuscripts (all English). See Tx No. 3: Bd Tx agree frequently, often in error.

10–11. **Fall of Troy**

fol. 89ra EXCIDIUM TROIE
(a) Pergama flere volo fato donais (*sic*) data solo
fol. 89vb (b) Viribus arte minis danaum data Troia ruinis
fol. 90rb . . . Vlcio pugnatur, fit machina, Troia crematur
EXPLICIT EXCIDIUM TROIE

(a) Walther 13985; ed. Hilka-Schumann, *Carmina Burana* No. 101 (1/2. 139–60); Bd has the full text, with no significant variants. (b) Walther 20582; ed. P. Leyser, *Historia poetarum et poematum medii aevi* (Halle, 1721), pp. 404–408; usually attributed to Peter of Saintes; Bd omits lines 187–200, 241–42, of the Leyser edition. These two poems are often found together without any sign of a break between them; Bd concludes with the couplet printed by Hilka-Schumann, p. 145. On the complex relationship between the poems and their textual affiliations, see Hilka-Schumann.

12. **John of Bridlington**

fol. 90rb (a) PROPHECIA CUIUSDAM DE DOMINO EDWARDO REGE ANGLIE TERCIO POST CONQUESTUM (*later hand (s. xv)*: secundum Io. de bridlington)
Febribus infectus requies fuerat michi lectus
fol. 94va . . . Ad mortem tendo morti mea carmina pendo

fol. 94va (b) VERSUS DE IIIIxx IIII
Cambri carnaruan anglis natum dabit agnum (*18 lines*)
. . .Hinc terrena spuens sanctus super ethera scandit

Walther 6296. Ed. Wright, *Political Poems* 1. 123–215. Bd has the verse text only, without the Ergom commentary; it lacks four lines of the text printed by Wright, but also has 29 extra lines. For a critical edition, see M.J. Curley, 'Versus propheciales, Prophecia Johannis Bridlingtoniensis', PhD diss. (Chicago, 1973). For a full study, see A.G. Rigg, 'John of Bridlington's *Prophecy*: a new look', *Speculum* 63 (1988), 596–613, in which I argue that John Ergom (whose commentary on the *Prophecy* was written 1362–64) was not the author of the poem, and that the poem was written about 1349–50. The verses 'Cambri carnaruan' are not part of the Bridlington prophecy, and are usually found (e.g. in Digby 186) with the title 'Versus de Gilde de Sexto Hibernico'. I am very grateful to Professor Michael J. Curley of the University of Puget Sound for advice on the poem.

13. Babio

fol. 94vb DE BABIONE ET CROCEO DOMINO BABIONIS ET VIOLA FILIASTRA BABIONIS QUAM CROCEUS DUXIT INVITO BABIONE ET PETULA VXORE BABIONIS ET FODIO SERVO EIUS. INCIPIT PREFACIO IN LIBRO BABIONIS
Me dolor infestat foris intus iugiter omnis
fol. 97va . . . Sunt incredibiles vxor alumpna cliens

Walther 10821. Ed. Andrea Dessì Fulgheri, in *Commedie latine del XII e XIII secolo*, II (Genoa, 1980), pp. 129–301. The author's final line is omitted: a space of four lines at the top of fol. 97vb may have been intended for the conclusion (or for a heading to No. 14).

14. Nigel Whiteacre: Speculum stultorum

fol. 97vb SPECULUM BURNELLI MERITO LIBER ISTE VOCATUR
CUIUS SUB SPECIE STULTORUM VITA NOTATUR
Suscipe pauca tui veteris Willelme Nigelli
fol. 114ra . . . Quam cum virtutum munera spreta iacent
BURNELLI DICTA MULTO MODERAMINE FICTA
SPERNERE QUI QUERIT SEMPER ASELLUS ERIT
fol. 114ra MORALITAS SPECULI BURNELLI
Dilecto et in christo diligendo . . .
fol. 115vb . . . cauterium admittant. EXPLICIT. AMEN

Walther 18944. Ed. J.H. Mozley and R.R. Raymo (Berkeley, 1960); 'Moralitas', i.e. Nigel's accompanying letter to William de Longchamps, ed. Mozley, *Medium aevum* 39 (1970) 13–20. For further bibliography, see Tx No. 1. Bd, Bodley 761, and Lambeth Palace 357 all have a lacuna 2483–3258 and end at 3448, and are thus in a separate family from Tx; of these three manuscripts only Bd has the prose 'moralitas'. On the textual tradition, see also Mozley, *Speculum* 4 (1929), 430–42, and 5 (1930), 251–63; A. Boutemy, *Speculum* 8 (1933), 510–

19; and K. Langosch, *Mittellateinisches Jahrbuch* 3 (1966), 280–6 (review of the Mozley-Raymo edition).

15. **Battle of Neville's Cross 1346**

fol. 116ra Corda superborum Scotorum destrue Christe
fol. 116vb . . . Spes tua conamen victoria lux releuamen

Walther 5041. Ed. Wright, *Political Poems* 1. 41–51, from BdTxRb (sole witnesses); see Tx No. 16, Rb No. 7(a) (*inc.* Dux Valeys). Bd lacks the first 26 lines and has many omissions, but has 20 extra lines at the end. For Rb's verse No. 7(c), see below, fly-leaf poem No. 43.

16. **Battle of Crécy 1346**

fol. 116vb Francia feminea pharisea vigoris ydea
fol. 118rb . . . Gloria solamen sit Christus in omnibus amen. Explicit

Walther 6833. Ed. Wright, *Political Poems* 1. 26–40, from BdTxRb (sole witnesses); see Tx No. 15, Rb No. 5(a). Bd differs slightly from the TxRb version.

17. **Verses**

fol. 118rb O niger intrusor et sancte sedis abusor,
Virginibus cede, presumpta sede recede:
Sufficiunt fures bini, non addito plures

Walther 12817, from Harley 3362 only. I suspect that the poem refers to the presence of friars (*niger intrusor* 'Dominican') in crucifixion scenes: see my *Glastonbury Miscellany* (Oxford, 1968), No. XXX, p. 78.

18. **Apocalypsis Goliae**

fol. 118va APOCALIPSIS MAGISTRI GALTERI MAHAP SUPER VITA ET MORIBUS PERSONARUM ECCLESIASTICARUM
A tauro torrida lampade cinthii
fol. 120vb . . . Mentis vestigia fecisset lubrica. Explicit

Walther 91. Ed. K. Strecker (Rome, 1928), using BdTx amongst others. See Tx No. 55, Rb No. 17.

19. **Riddle**

fol. 120vb Que noua praua nimis peiora nouissima primis;
Rex venit et sua gens nil probitatis agens.
Litera bina mei conprehendit nomen amici,
Montibus vna salit, maxillas altera tegit

Walther 15015; unique. I have not solved it.

20. **Vitalis of Blois: Geta**

fol. 120vb INCIPIT COMEDIA DE GETA. PROLOGUS

(C)armina composuit voluitque placere poeta
fol. 123ra ... Birria geta hominem se fore, queque placent

Walther 7272. Ed. Ferruccio Bertini, in *Commedie latine del XII e XIII secolo*, III (Genoa, 1980), pp. 139–242. See Tx No. 51. Scribe: Dodsthorp (cf. fol. 5r–v). Fol. 123v blank.

Part III: fols 124–208

Piers Plowman

fol. 124r (a) In a somer sesoun wen softe was the sonne
fol. 139r ... Here penaunce ant here purgatorye vpon thys puyr erthe.
fol. 139r (b) Pers quad a prest tho þi pardoun most I rede ...
fol. 140v ... To vs and alle cristin God leue it so byfalle. Amen
Explicit vita et visio Petri Plowman
fol. 141r (c) Thus y robed in russet y romed aboute
fol. 208r ... And seþe he gradde after grace tyl y gan awake
Explicit passus secundus de Dobest

(a) Z-version, ed. Rigg-Brewer; (b) Q^1 continuation, ed. Rigg-Brewer; (c) C-text. On these versions see Brewer, above, pp. 13–20. A line from *Piers Plowman* is written by Dodsthorp on fol. 3r (No. 54), but it was not copied directly from Bd (where it appears on fol. 126v).

fol. 208v A list, written by Dodsthorp, of seventeen abbey officials (e.g. *celerarius, camerarius*) or officials of dependent houses (e.g. *Prior Sancti Iuonis, Custos Bernuel*), with small sums of money against each name (e.g. *Infirmarius ij s. ij d.*) The presence on the list of 'Ranulphi abbatis' (abbot 1231–53) suggests that the list may be of sums of money assigned for specific monastic purposes (in Ranulph's case, perhaps for an office in his name).

APPENDIX: fols 1–4

This extra quire of fly-leaves (not included in the final series of quire numbers) may have been added by Dodsthorp, the final compiler of the manuscript. Nos. 22–45 (fol. 2v) and 53 and 55 (on fol. 3r) had already been written when Dodsthorp began to make his own entries. He filled fol. 2r and the remainder of fols 2v and 3r, and wrote at least one of the poems on fol. 4v; the rest was left blank (fol. 1r was later used by librarians). There are over seventy items, a few English or French but most Latin; the mixture is typical of fly-leaf poetry of the period: there are items of local interest, riddles, proverbs, literary extracts, drinking and begging poems, etc. Some entries are difficult to read and decipher; others are obscure in themselves. Bibliographical details (where known to me) are given in the notes which follow; reference is made to the *Index of Middle English Verse* (New York, 1943) by C. Brown and R.H. Robbins, and the

Supplement (Lexington, Ky., 1965) by Robbins and J.L. Cutler. I have silently corrected minor slips (such as extra minims) and ignored cancelled words and letters.

fol. 2r

1 Si capud est, currit; ventrem sibi iunge, volabit;
Adde pedem, comede, vel sine ventre, bibe. Muscatum
2 Est puer inberbis sine sensu, non sine verbis.
3 O benedicte pie, prece virginis alme marie,
Venturis annis Wellis memorare Iohannis:
Doctor erat gratus, prudens, pius, hic tumulatus,
Moribus ornatus, venerans fuit et veneratus.
4 Salue, Tyrel, salue, salueris, episcope calue.
5 Est tua vel cuius? Mea non, sed pauperis huius.
6 Allea, vina, venus, puluis, ventus, faba, fumus:
Ista nocent oculis, sed vigilare magis. quod dodissethorp
7 Wlnera quater centum sunt Christi milia quinque . . . (*4 lines*)
Nota secundum eusebium tot wlnera Christus habuit: quinque milia quatraginta 1x^{a} et quindecim
8 Ori quinque placent; si quatuor, aere pendent;
Si tria, pes homini; si duo dulce sonat. dapes
9 Quod fueram non sum – barbam, capud aspice tonsum –
Huc veni; noli credulus esse doli. vlpes
Vestis honesta quidem, sed quod fuerat tibi pridem
Est cor semper idem: cur dare nolo fidem! galina
10 Insipiens, seruus, nuptus quoque, racio, morbus.
11 Wlgus vel monachi, mulieres siue caballi,
Cum peregrinantur, peiores efficiuntur.
12 Vt te collaudem, fac fraudem fallere fraudem;
Cum, fraus fraude perit, laus tibi maior erit.
13 Calciamenta peto tua, sunt mea fracta, videto!
14 Hic fons, fons ille, tibi mentum more sibille, etc.
15 Nuncius istorum ter quinquaginta pirorum
Si numerum minuat, corpore queso luat! dodisth'
16 Promittebatur capo sed gallina dabatur;
Quod fuit auca heri, modo wlt vt sinus haberi. o quod dod'
17 Christe, Dei verbum, michi pectus tolle superbum.
18 Versis retro pilis iuuenescit calua senilis;
Retrofacta scisma causatur fronte sophisma.
19 Simplex prelatus fuit Odo þe gode vocatus;
Pro bonitate modo manet in celestibus Odo.

2 Written in margin. 3 See above, p. 29. *prudens* written twice, first cancelled. 4 I can find no record of a Bishop Tyrel. 5 Walther 5875. 6 *Sprichwörter* 810. 8 Walther 13475. 9 Walther 16259. 10 *racio* glossed *.i. debitor*; margin: *Monachi ex* . . . (illegible). 12 Cf. Ovid. *Ars amatoria* 3. 491: repeated as No. 60 below. 16 *sinus* = *cygnus*. 17 Cf. Walther 2688. 18 Obscure. 19 Odo, archbishop of Canterbury, died 959.

20 Be God and seynt Hillare . . . (*2 stanzas, aaab aaab*)
21 Pontificum spuma michi mantellum sine pluma . . . (*6 lines*)
22 O tu gauter vandr . . .
23 In primo scribas va. qui scribere curas. Nota sonat puer alta silet cras sit tibi merces si capud abstuleris /. . . vanum dico laboras
24 Sermo propheta ius fur piger et medicina Immemor accusans rex heremita iubet
25 Intus quis? Ego sum. Quid queris? Vt intrem.
Fers aliquid? Non. Esto foris. Fero quid. Satis, intra!
26 Seruos seruiles solebat dicere miles
Clericos claustrales monachus sed imperiales.
27 A potu primo pectus purgatur ab ymo . . . (*11 lines*)
28 Si bene perpendi sunt cause quinque bibendi:
Hospitis aduentus, presens sitis atque futura,
Occasus solis, et ne pereant mea iura.
Egrotare potes, nisi vinum post pira potes.
29 Falco pica lupus casellum cor leue lutus;
Sic docet astutum cor retinere suum.
30 Auctor amoris ait Naso, pars maxima rerum
Offenditur si non interiora tegas etc.
31 Ve tibi mi siate modicum quia defluit a te . . . (*5 lines*)
32 In cratere meo tetus est coniuncta leeo . . . (*4 lines*)
33 O tu pincerna qui seruicie dominaris . . . (*4 lines*)
34 Da vinum docto, stulto laico de flumine cocto.
35 Plus puero puer es pueris qui totus adheres:
Dum pueris heres, comoda pauca feres.
36 Symonis exemplo sint prelati bene tuti:
Tucius in templo quam regum curribus vti.
37 Si cur quando fuge; tibi sint . . . nisi nuge
Freni vel vestis attraccio sit tibi testis.
38 Sunt duo Iacobi, Iacobus minor et Iacob ibi:
Maior habet baculum, sed minor non timet illum.
39 Dum potes, esto dator; post te veniet dominator . . . (*4 lines*)
40 Pauperis et regis communis lex moriendi . . . (*6 lines*)
41 Gallicus: Mortuus est brunus, non viuit forcior vnus.
Anglicus: Tantum sed mille meliores quam fuit ille.

20 *Index*, No. 569; printed by T. Wright and J.O. Halliwell, *Reliquiae antiquae*, 2 vols (London, 1841–43). 1. 259 'The Madman's Song', with No. 42 below. 21 Walther 14264; ed. C.J. McDonough, *The Oxford Poems of Hugh Primas and the Arundel Lyrics* (Toronto, 1984), p. 30. Bd has lines 1a, 2b, 9–10 (altered), 13, 23, 2a + 1b. 22–23 illegible. 24 Obscure. 25 Walther 9518. 26 Obscure. 27 Cf. Walther 9052 (and *Appendix*); Rigg, *Glastonbury Miscellany*, p. 65: Bd differs slightly. 28 Walther 17624 (and *Appendix*); '5' before *cause*. 29 The fable of the wolf, the crow, and the cheese. 30 Ovid, *Ars amatoria* 3. 229–30. 31 Walther 20000; *siate* = *cyathe*. 32 Walther 8870; ed. Meyer, *Primas*, No. 14; *Carmina Burana* 1. 3, No. 194(i); *tetus* = *Thetis*. 33 Walther 13017 (and *Appendix*); printed from Harley 3362 in *Zeitschrift für deutsches Altertum* 84 (1953) 268; *seruicie* = *cerevisiae*. 34 *Sprichörter* 4865. 37 Obscure. 39 Walther 4924. 40 Walther 13873, *Sprichwörter* 20987.

42 I am a hert, I am no are . . . (*2 stanzas, aabb ccbb*)
43 Est omnis Scotus Samson, Salamon, leo totus . . . (*3 lines*)
44 Est venia coruis grauis censura columbis.
45 Spend and God send, alleluia; spare and go bare, tristicia.
46 Hoc opus expleui sub primi floribus eui;
Cum maior fuerit mundus minor et alter erit.
47 Summa . . . Laus Deo, pax viuis, requies eterna defunctis.
48 Thomas de Burgo cum wltu spectat alurgo.
49 Fallere gnarus homo Norfolchica venit ab humo.
50 Yuo transiuit rector dormit cap. . viuit
51 Retro pilis versis tibi basia coserat ers his.
52 Q. Premor et puer es, cur collo tam grauis heres?
Non lateat tibi res – quem fers est celicus heres.

fol. 3r

53 Ieo fas iose a suffler de set had mot gens . . . mester.
54 Chastite wihtout charite brennit in helle
55 Io fasse de se que droyt est . . .
56 Vita breuis casusque leuis nec spes remeandi . . . (*4 lines*)
quod dodisthorp
57 Qui fratres odis, quos verba per aspera prodis,
Tu Iudam sequeris et Iudas alter haberis. quod dodisth'
58 Pauper homo letus, fortunam fronte salutat,
Et cum nil habeat, nil sibi deesse putat. quod dodisth'
59 Qui me corrodunt saltem post fata silebunt.
60 Vt te collaudem fac fraudem fallere fraudem;
Cum fraus fraude perit, laus tibi maior erit. quod dodisth'
61 Hic canis est Fordam, hic collum da sibi cordam.
62 Hoc bis non datur menp set sepc' nominettur
63 Lauti laudate, dicunt miseri miserere, etc. quod dodisth'
64 Profuit ad meritum tendere colla grui.
65 Nato de scorto pira porto cum pede torto.
66 Nota: quatuor erant socii componentes hos versus de duabus situlis pendentibus iuxta fontem, variatis versibus, sentencia non variata, etc.:
Hee situle pendent bibule variant vice prima:
Cum redit ebrea pars sua sobria tendit ad yma.
Hee situle pendent patule variant vice versa:
Retrogradum petit vna gratum, redit altera mersa.

42 Printed as the second half of 'The Madman's Song': see No. 20 above; there is no reason to connect the two poems. 43 Walther 5786; see Rb No. 7(c). 45 *Index* and *Supplement* 3209, without Bd. 46 Glossed *opus* 'mundus', *expleui* 'compleui', *minor* 's. mundus'. 49 Cf. Tx No. 64, Rb No. 24; *humo*: MS. *huimo*. 50 St Ives was a dependent house of Ramsey. 51 Obscure. 52 St Christopher: see above, p. 24. 53, 55 Drawings of man with sickle; both lines illegible. 54 *Piers Plowman* B-text. 1. 817 (Bd fol. 126v): the variant *brennit* (for *worth cheyned*) is not recorded elsewhere. 56 Walther 20660 (and *Appendix*); *nota bene et . . .* in margin. 57 *Sprichwörter* 24100, 24101; in margin: *Nota pallee non dantur sed consueta opera exiguntur*. 58 MS. *frontem*. 60 See no. 12 above. 61 Probably nothing to do with the Fordam who was bishop of Durham 1382–88 and of Ely 1388–1425. 62 Obscure. 64 *Babio* 12. 65 *Sprichwörter* 15920 (Juvenal).

Haustra pericula, maxime pendula, bina notescunt:
Dant simul obuia fronte crudelia, nec requiescunt.
Hausta gemella vicem, potandi pendula mutant:
Dum saciata Iouem, tedidem vacuata salutant.

67 Ad varios fines vario de vertice crines
Vertit ricardus ne pereat ipse pilardus.

68 Cama canis parcus cornu catapulta vir archus

69 Pre. mia. vi. tis. datur hanc mors dira f. vitis

70 Hec sunt signa theos: aquila, vir, leo, bos.

71 Episcopus in textu loquitur canonico:
Bestia que tangit montem lapidis ruit ictu;
Hoc quid sit dictu, frater carissime, dic tu.
Canonicus respondet in glosa episcopo:
Bestia canonicus mons femina pontificalis
Ex ictu lapidis priuacio canonicalis.

72 Pro meritis vite dedit illi laurea nomen;
Detur ei vite laurea pro meritis.

73 Si omnes forent fideles minime valerent lokeris and laweris.

74 Qui super es tu qui superes successor honoris
Degeneres si degeneres a laude prioris.

75 Roma breuis scitur testudine dum sepelitur,
Itur, reditur, nescitur vbi reperitur.
Sarcina Walteri iuuenes premit et tulit
Willelme velut . . . conuenient veteri.

fol. 4v

76 Francisco fundente preces vt tempore multo . . . (8 *lines*)

77 Wan gonaway chal on curteis calle . . . (8 *lines*)

78 *Table of consanguinity*

67–69 Obscure. 73–75 in margin. 74 Cf. *Sprichwörter* 24839a. 75 Obscure. 76 Walther 6844. 77 *Index Supplement* 3951.5: ed. R.H. Robbins, *Historical Poems of the Fourteenth and Fifteenth Centuries* (New York, 1959), pp. 316–17.

Bibliography

Adams, Robert. 'Editing *Piers Plowman* B: The Imperative of an Intermittently Critical Edition'. *Studies in Bibliography* 45 (1992): 31–68.

———. Review of Rigg and Brewer. *Studies in the Age of Chaucer* 7 (1985): 233–237.

Allen, Judson Boyce. 'Langland's Reading and Writing: *Detractor* and the Pardon Passus'. *Speculum* 59 (1984): 342–62.

Brewer, Charlotte. 'The Textual Principles of Kane's A Text'. *Yearbook of Langland Studies* 3 (1989): 67–90.

———. 'Authorial vs. Scribal Writing in *Piers Plowman*'. *Medieval Literature*. Ed. T.W. Machan. Binghamton, New York, 1991. 59–89.

———. 'George Kane's Processes of Revision'. *Crux and Controversy*. Ed. A.J. Minnis and Charlotte Brewer. Cambridge, UK, 1992. 71–92.

Chambers, R.W., and Grattan, J.H.G. 'The Text of *Piers Plowman*'. *Modern Language Review* 4 (1909): 357–89.

———. 'The Text of *Piers Plowman*: Critical Methods'. *Modern Language Review* 11 (1916): 257–275.

Clark, David Lee (ed.). *Shelley's Prose*. London, 1988.

Coffman, George R. 'The Present State of a Critical Edition of *Piers Plowman*'. *Speculum* 20 (1945): 482–3.

Crowley, Robert (ed.). *The Vision of Pierce Plowman*. 3 editions. London, 1550.

DiMarco, Vincent. 'The Authorship of *Piers Plowman*'. *Anglia* 100 (1982): 124–9.

Donaldson, E.T. 'MSS R and F in the B Tradition of *Piers Plowman*'. *Transactions of the Connecticut Academy of Arts and Sciences* 39 (1955): 177–212.

———. 'The Texts of *Piers Plowman*: Scribes and Poets'. *Modern Philology* 50 (1952–3): 269–73.

Duggan, Hoyt N. 'The Authenticity of the Z-text of *Piers Plowman*: Further Notes on Metrical Evidence'. *Medium Ævum* 56 (1987): 25–45.

Emden, A.B. *A Biographical Register of the University of Oxford to 1500*. 3 vols. Oxford, 1957–59.

Garnett, Richard. 'Antiquarian Book Clubs'. *Quarterly Review* 164 (1848): 309–42.

Grattan, J.H.G. 'The Critical Edition of *Piers Plowman*: Its Present Status'. *Speculum* 26 (1951): 582–3.

Green, Richard Firth. Review of Rigg and Brewer. *Analytical and Enumerative Bibliography* 8 (1984): 129–133.

———. 'The Lost Exemplar of the Z-Text of *Piers Plowman* and its 20-Line Pages'. *Medium Ævum* 56 (1987): 307–309.

Hudson, Anne. 'The Variable Text'. *Crux and Controversy*. Ed. A.J. Minnis and Charlotte Brewer. Cambridge, UK, 1992. 49–60.

Hussey, S.S. 'Eighty Years of *Piers Plowman* Scholarship: A Study of Critical Methods'. University of London, M.A. dissertation (unpublished), 1952.

James, M.R. (ed.). *Walter Map. De Nugis Curialium*. Anecdota Oxoniensia, Med. and Mod. Ser. 14. Oxford, 1914.

———. Brooke, C.N.L., and Mynors, R.A.B. (eds.). *Walter Map. De Nugis Curialium*. Oxford, 1983.

Kane, George (ed.). '*Piers Plowman*': *The A Version*. London, 1960.

———, and Donaldson, E.T. (eds.). '*Piers Plowman*': *The B Version*. London, 1975.

———. 'The "Z Version" of *Piers Plowman*'. *Speculum* 60 (1985): 910–30.

———. 'The Text.' *A Companion to Piers Plowman*. Ed. John A. Alford. Berkeley and Los Angeles, 1988. 175–200.

King, John. *English Reformation Literature*. Princeton, 1982.

Knott, Thomas A., and Fowler, David C. (eds.). *Piers the Plowman: A Critical Edition of the A-Version*. Baltimore, 1952.

Machan, T.W. 'Late Middle English Texts and the Higher and Lower Criticisms'. *Medieval Literature*. Ed. T.W. Machan. Binghamton, New York, 1991. 3–15.

———. 'Middle English Text Production and Modern Textual Criticism'. *Crux and Controversy*. Ed. A.J. Minnis and Charlotte Brewer. Cambridge, UK, 1992. 1–38.

Madan, F.H., and Craster, H.H.E. *A Summary Catalogue of Western Manuscripts in the Bodleian Library at Oxford*. Vol. 2. Oxford, 1922.

Manly, J.M. 'The Lost Leaf of Piers the Plowman'. *Modern Philology* 3 (1906): 359–366.

Middleton, Anne. 'XVIII. *Piers Plowman*'. *A Manual of the Writings in Middle English 1050–1500*. Vol. 7. Ed. Albert E. Hartung. New Haven, 1986: 2211–34, 2417–43.

Nichol, Henry. 'An Account of M. Gaston Paris's Method of Editing in his *Vie de Saint Alexis*'. *Transactions of the Philological Society* (1977–8–9): 339–40.

Patterson, Lee. 'The Logic of Textual Criticism and the Way of Genius: The Kane-Donaldson *Piers Plowman* in Historical Perspective'. *Negotiating the Past*. Lee Patterson. Madison, Wisconsin, 1987. 77–113.

Pearsall, Derek. 'The Ilchester Manuscript of *Piers Plowman*'. *Neuphilologische Mitteilungen* 82 (1981): 181–93.

———. Review of Rigg and Brewer. *Archiv* 222 (1985): 181–184.

Rigg, A.G. *A Glastonbury Miscellany of the Fifteenth Century*. Oxford, 1968.

———. 'Medieval Latin Poetic Anthologies (I)'. *Medieval Studies* 39 (1977): 281–330.

———. 'Medieval Latin Poetic Anthologies (II)'. *Medieval Studies* 40 (1978): 387–407.

———. 'Medieval Latin Poetic Anthologies (III)'. *Medieval Studies* 41 (1979): 468–505.

———. *Gawain on marriage: the textual tradition of the 'De coniuge non ducenda' with critical edition and translation*. Toronto 1986.

———. 'John of Bridlington's *Prophecy*: a new look'. *Speculum* 63 (1988): 596–613.

Rigg, A.G., and Brewer, Charlotte (eds.). '*Piers Plowman*': *The Z Version*. Toronto, 1983.

Ritson, Joseph. *Bibliographia Poetica: a Catalogue of English Poets of the Twelfth, Thirteenth, Fourteenth, Fifteenth, and Sixteenth Centurys, with a short account of their works*. London, 1802.

Scase, Wendy. 'Two *Piers Plowman* C-Text Interpolations: Evidence for a Second Textual Tradition'. *Notes and Queries* 34 (1987): 456–63.
Schmidt, A.V.C. 'The Authenticity of the Z Text of *Piers Plowman*: A Metrical Examination'. *Medium Ævum* 53 (1984): 295–300.
Skeat, Rev. Walter W. (ed.). *The Romans of Lancelot of the Laik*. EETS, os 6 (1865).
———. (ed.). *Parallel Extracts from Twenty-nine Manuscripts of Piers Plowman* . . . EETS, os 17 (1866).
———. *The Vision of William concerning Piers Plowman* . . . *The "Vernon" Text; or Text A*. EETS, os 28 (1867).
———. (ed.). *The Vision of William concerning Piers Plowman* . . . *The 'Crowley' Text; or Text B*. EETS, os 38 (1869).
———. (ed.). *The Vision of William concerning Piers Plowman* . . . *The 'Whitaker' Text; or Text C*. EETS, os 54 (1873).
———. (ed.). *The Vision of William concerning Piers Plowman* . . . *Notes to Texts A, B, and C*. EETS, os 67 (1885 for 1877).
———. (ed.). *The Vision of William concerning Piers Plowman* . . . *General Preface, Notes, and Indexes*. EETS, os 81 (1885 for 1884).
———. (ed.). *The Vision of William concerning Piers Plowman in Three Parallel Texts* . . . 2 vols. Oxford, 1886.
———. *A Student's Pastime*. Oxford, 1896.
Sweet, Henry. Sixth Annual Address of the President to the Philological Society. *Transactions of the Philological Society* (1977–8–9): 10–16.
Tyrwhitt, Thomas (ed.). *The Canterbury Tales of Chaucer*. 5 vols. London, 1775–8.
Warton, Thomas. *The History of English Poetry from the Close of the Eleventh to the Commencement of the Eighteenth Century*. Ed. Richard Price. London, 1824.
Whitaker, Thomas Dunham (ed.). *Visio Willelmi de Petro Plouhman Item Visiones ejusdem de Dowel, Dobet, et Dobest or, The Vision of William concerning Piers Plouhman* . . . London, 1813.
White, Hugh. Review of Rigg and Brewer. *Medium Ævum* 53 (1984): 290–294.
Wright, Thomas (ed.). *The Vision and the Creed of Piers Ploughman*. 2 vols. London, 1842; revised ed. 1856.
[Wright, Thomas.] 'The Visions of Piers Plowman'. *Gentleman's Magazine* n.s. 1: 385–91.

MS/ARCHIVE MATERIAL

Letters and Papers

Chambers Papers, University College London
Skeat-Furnivall Papers, Kings College London
Bradshaw Letters, Cambridge University Library

Manuscripts cited

Piers Plowman

A-Texts
Cambridge, Trinity College MS R.3.14 (T)
Oxford, Bodleian Library MS Eng.poet.a.1 (the 'Vernon manuscript') (V)

Oxford, Bodleian Library MS Douce 323 (SC 21897) (D)
Oxford, Bodleian Library MS Ashmole 1468 (SC 7004) (A)
London, Lincoln's Inn Library MS 150 (L)
London, British Library MS Harley 3954 (H^3)
London, British Library MS Harley 875 (H)
Oxford, University College MS 45 (held in the Bodleian Library) (U)

A- + C-Texts
London, British Library MS Harley 6041 (H^2)
Oxford, Bodleian Library MS Digby 145 (SC 1746) (K)

B-Texts
Cambridge, Trinity College MS B.15.17 (W)
Oxford, Oriel College MS 79 (in the Bodleian) (O)
Oxford, Bodleian Library MS Laud Misc. 581 (SC 987) (L)
Oxford, Bodleian Library MS Rawlinson Poetry 38 (SC 15563) (R)
London, British Library MS Additional 10574 (Bm)
Oxford, Corpus Christi College MS 201 (F)
London, British Library MS Cotton Caligula A.XI(2) (Cot)

C-Texts
San Marino, Huntington Library MS HM 137 (*olim* Phillipps 8231) (P)
London, University of London Sterling Library MS V.88 (the Ilchester MS) (I)
Cambridge University Library MS Ff.5.35 (F)

Mixed Texts
Oxford, Bodleian Library MS Bodley 851 (SC 3041) (Z or Bd)
San Marino, Huntington Library MS HM 114 (*olim* Phillipps 8252) (Ht)

Other MSS (selected list)
Cambridge, Trinity College MS 0.9.38 (Ty)
London, British Library MS Cotton Titus A.xx (Tx)
London, British Library MS Cotton Vespasian E.xii (Ve)
Oxford, Bodleian Library MS Add. A.44 (the Bekynton Anthology)
Oxford, Bodleian Library MS Bodley 603 (B)
Oxford, Bodleian Library MS Digby 166 (D)
Oxford, Bodleian Library MS Rawlinson B.214 (Rb)

Facsimile

Venit amicus ia prima genus [illegible]
[illegible] vigor clamitat [illegible]
[illegible] speculo [illegible] placet velana [illegible]
Qui videt hanc [illegible] sibi
Hic sibi [illegible] vocat [illegible] subito [illegible]
[illegible] digna videt [illegible] videre stupet
Hospitis aula [illegible]
[illegible]

Et primus thalamo teste pu[illegible] amor
Vespres soror [illegible] et rapit ipse
Sed [illegible] [illegible] sic amicus [illegible]
Sed soror [illegible] [illegible] hoste
Sed soror [illegible] ipse cubile [illegible]
[illegible] hic [illegible] [illegible] [illegible] [illegible]
[illegible] [illegible] [illegible] [illegible] timet [illegible] timor
Hic redit et dulces [illegible] [illegible] [illegible]
[illegible] [illegible] [illegible] [illegible] [illegible] [illegible]
Sene volat [illegible] [illegible] a [illegible]
Vt [illegible] [illegible] [illegible] blandi[illegible]
[illegible] et ditat ab [illegible] munere [illegible]
[illegible] munit [illegible] [illegible] [illegible] [illegible]
[illegible] sibi [illegible] opes [illegible] [illegible] [illegible]
[illegible] [illegible] [illegible] forma [illegible] [illegible]
[illegible] sibi vix [illegible] vix [illegible] [illegible]
[illegible] [illegible] [illegible] pene fides
[illegible] fidei [illegible] [illegible] [illegible]
[illegible] [illegible] latebras [illegible] ille [illegible]
[illegible] tenebris [illegible] ipse [illegible] [illegible] [illegible]
Signa [illegible] [illegible] signa [illegible] [illegible]
[illegible] dolet [illegible] [illegible] hec dolet
[illegible] dolor iste dolo [illegible] amat arte dolus
Laudat [illegible] et [illegible] [illegible] plus laudat amat
Sic [illegible] hoc [illegible] [illegible] [illegible] [illegible] monet
Sic [illegible] hoc [illegible] [illegible] [illegible] illa [illegible]
[illegible] [illegible] pulsat hostia pellet [illegible]
[illegible] [illegible] [illegible] [illegible] [illegible] illa
[illegible] [illegible] [illegible] [illegible] [illegible]
[illegible] [illegible] [illegible] [illegible] [illegible] [illegible]
Sic [illegible] [illegible] [illegible] [illegible] [illegible]
[illegible] [illegible] [illegible] mechus ne latebat
An lateat mechus [illegible] [illegible] latet
[illegible] [illegible] [illegible] [illegible] [illegible] [illegible]
[illegible] [illegible] [illegible] [illegible] [illegible] [illegible]
Vix [illegible] [illegible] [illegible] pellere [illegible]
[illegible] [illegible] [illegible] perdere [illegible] [illegible]
[illegible] timor [illegible] [illegible] [illegible] [illegible]
Hinc timet hinc [illegible] [illegible] [illegible] timore
[illegible] timet [illegible] [illegible] [illegible] [illegible]
[illegible] [illegible] [illegible] [illegible] [illegible] [illegible]
Sic [illegible] [illegible] [illegible] [illegible] [illegible]
Sic [illegible] timet [illegible] [illegible]
Hinc [illegible] hinc [illegible] [illegible] [illegible] [illegible]
Obliquus [illegible] [illegible] [illegible] [illegible]
[illegible] [illegible] [illegible] [illegible] [illegible] dolos
[illegible] [illegible] [illegible] [illegible] [illegible]
[illegible] [illegible] [illegible] fraudes [illegible] [illegible]
[illegible] [illegible] [illegible] [illegible] [illegible] [illegible]
[illegible] [illegible] [illegible] [illegible] [illegible]
[illegible] vt [illegible] dulce [illegible] [illegible]

[illegible] [illegible] [illegible] [illegible] dolet [illegible]
Sit dolus ille dolor [illegible] [illegible] [illegible] [illegible]
[illegible] tegit [illegible] est [illegible] [illegible] [illegible]
[illegible] plus [illegible] [illegible] plus [illegible] [illegible]
[illegible] [illegible] [illegible] [illegible] [illegible] [illegible]
[illegible] ille [illegible] [illegible] [illegible] [illegible] amat [illegible]
[illegible] [illegible] [illegible] [illegible] [illegible] amor
[illegible] [illegible] ipse [illegible] [illegible] [illegible] [illegible]
[illegible] [illegible] [illegible] [illegible] talia [illegible] [illegible]
[illegible] [illegible] [illegible] [illegible] [illegible] [illegible]
[illegible] [illegible] [illegible] [illegible] ipse [illegible]
Ipsa legit [illegible] tenebras qua [illegible] [illegible]
[illegible] qua [illegible] [illegible] amat [illegible] [illegible]
[illegible] [illegible] [illegible] [illegible] [illegible] [illegible]
Illa [illegible] [illegible] [illegible] ab [illegible] [illegible]
[illegible] [illegible] [illegible] [illegible] [illegible] [illegible]
[illegible] [illegible] [illegible] [illegible] moneta [illegible]
Hic [illegible] [illegible] [illegible] [illegible] gaudia [illegible]
Est [illegible] [illegible] [illegible] [illegible] [illegible]
[illegible] [illegible] [illegible] ille [illegible] [illegible] [illegible]
[illegible] [illegible] [illegible] plurima plura [illegible]
Plura dabit [illegible] plura dedit [illegible] [illegible]
[illegible] latebris [illegible] [illegible] [illegible]
Hic [illegible] ille [illegible] [illegible] [illegible] [illegible]
[illegible] [illegible] [illegible] [illegible] [illegible] [illegible]
[illegible] [illegible] [illegible] [illegible] [illegible] [illegible]
[illegible] [illegible] [illegible] [illegible] [illegible] [illegible]
[illegible] [illegible] [illegible] [illegible] [illegible] [illegible]
Ianua pallet [illegible] [illegible] [illegible] [illegible]
[illegible] [illegible] [illegible] [illegible] [illegible] [illegible]
[illegible] [illegible] mechum [illegible] [illegible] [illegible]
[illegible] [illegible] [illegible] [illegible] [illegible] [illegible]
[illegible] [illegible] [illegible] [illegible] [illegible] [illegible]
[illegible] illa [illegible] [illegible] [illegible] [illegible]
[illegible] [illegible] [illegible] ille [illegible]
[illegible] [illegible] [illegible] [illegible] [illegible] [illegible]
Hic [illegible] [illegible] [illegible] [illegible] ille [illegible]
[illegible] [illegible] [illegible] [illegible] [illegible] [illegible]
[illegible] [illegible] [illegible] [illegible] [illegible] [illegible]
[illegible] [illegible] [illegible] [illegible] [illegible] [illegible]
[illegible] [illegible] [illegible] [illegible] [illegible] [illegible]
[illegible] [illegible] [illegible] [illegible] [illegible] [illegible]
[illegible] [illegible] latebris [illegible] [illegible] [illegible]
Rex vigilat [illegible] [illegible] [illegible] [illegible] [illegible]
[illegible] [illegible] [illegible] [illegible] [illegible] [illegible]
[illegible] [illegible] [illegible] [illegible] [illegible] [illegible]
[illegible] [illegible] [illegible] [illegible] [illegible] [illegible]
[illegible] [illegible] porta [illegible] [illegible] [illegible] [illegible]
[illegible] tegit mechum [illegible] [illegible] [illegible] [illegible]
[illegible] [illegible] porta [illegible] [illegible] [illegible]

Hic redit ad [illegible] [illegible] [illegible] [illegible] [illegible] liber [illegible] [illegible] [illegible] [illegible] [illegible]

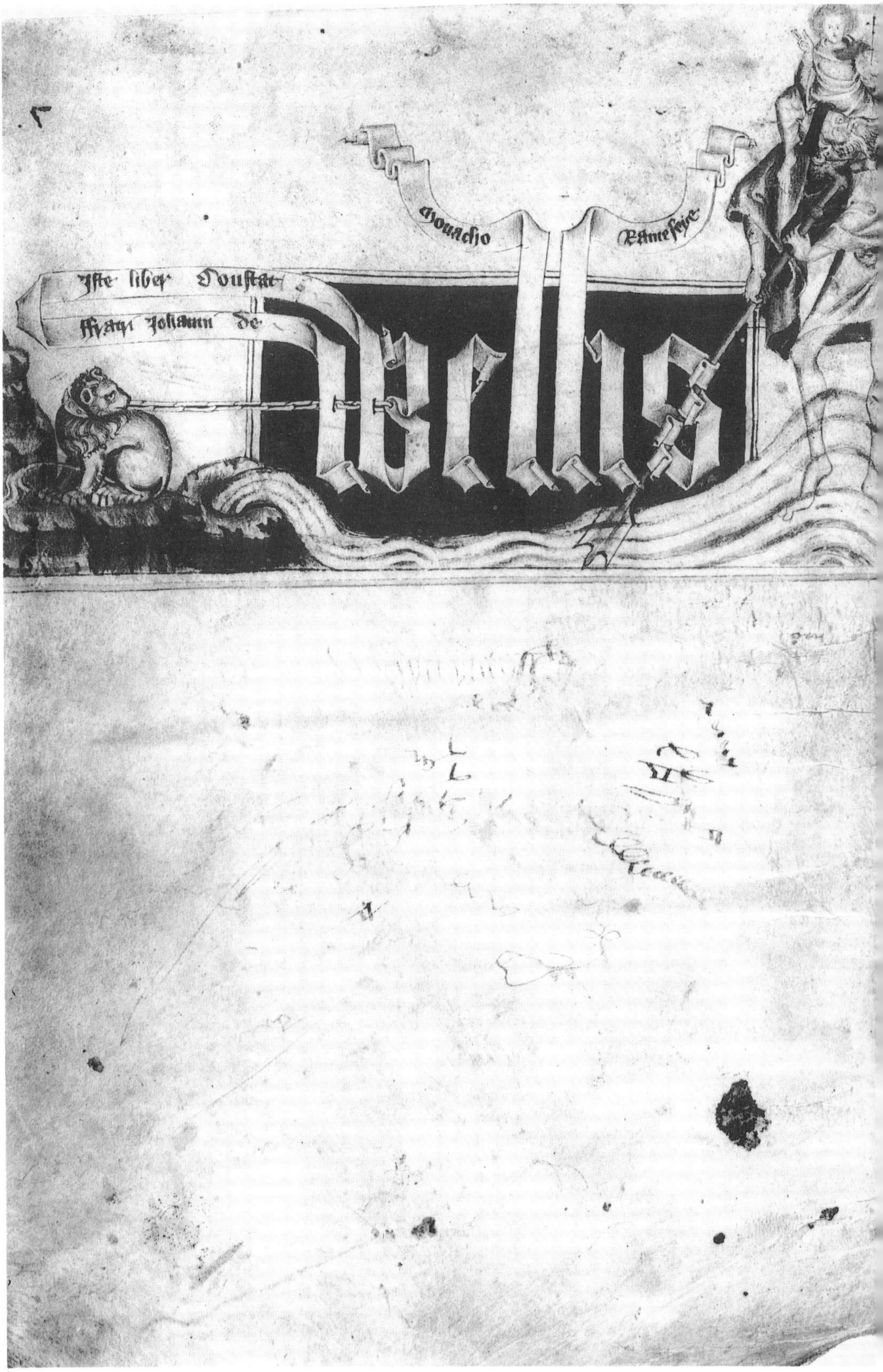
Iste liber constat
ffratri Johanni de
Wellis
Monacho
Rameseye

In a somer sesoun whon softe was the sonne
y schop me in to a schroud as y a scheep were
In abite as an hermite vnholy of werkes
Wente wyde in this world wondres to here
And sey many sellys y can nat sey alle
Ac in a May morwen vnder Malverne hylles
Me bifel a ferly of fayre me thoughte
I was wery of wandret and wente me to reste
vnder a brod bych by a born syde
And as y lay and lened and loked in the water
I slumbred in a slep hit sweyed so myre
Thenne gan y meten a merveylouse swevene
That y was in a wyldernesse wyst y never where
As y by-held in the est an hey to the sonne
I sey a tour on a toft tryelich y maked
A dep dale by nethe as dim as a cloude
Hit thondred as me thouzte tho and nawher elles
A fayre feld ful of folk fond y there by twene
Of alle maner men bothe mene and ryche
Werchyng and wandryng as the world asketh
Summe pute hem to the plough pleyden ful selde
In settyng and sowyng swonken ful harde
Wonne that wastors with glotenye destruyen
Summe pute hem to pruide parayled hem ther after
In contynaunce in clothinge come degised
In preyeres and in penaunces putte hem monye
Al for love of ure lord leveden ful streyte
Al for hope to have heveneriche blysse
As ankres and hermites that holdeth hem in here sellys
Coveyteth nat in contreye to kayren aboute
For no likerouse liflode here licam to plese
And summe chosen chaffare cheveden the bettre
As hit semeth to oure syght that suche men y thryveth
And summe murthes to make as mynstrales cunneth
nolle noyth swynke ne swete but swere grete othes
And as here licam loveth leveth there after
Bydderes as beggares faste a boute yede
Tyl here bagges and here balies were ful y crammed
Faytede for here fode and foughten at the ale
In glotonye god wot goth they to bedde
And ryseth with ribaudye tho roberdes knaves
Slep and sleuthe seweth hem evere
ffreres y fond there of alle foure ordres
Preched the puple for profit of the wombe
Glosed the gospel as hem good liked
For coveytise of copes construed hit as they wolde
Hermytes on an heep with hoked staves
Wente to Walsingham and here wenches after
Pylegrymes and palmeres plihten hem to gyderes
To seint Jemes of Galis & seyntes of Rome.

Wenten forth on here way wt many wyse tales
And haveden leve to lye al here lyf after
Bisshopes blessed there beren here staves
Seden synguliche here offices y deme hem neen other
For tho apostles to plaas apendeth here stat
And so y leve they love and lere us the same
Religious to yome yonne in a yonte
To a propre personages that pore clerkis hasketh
Barones and burgeys and bondage also
y say in that semble as ye schal here
here after persones and persthe prestes preye here bisschop
For here parisshes were so pore seth the pestilence tyme
To have a licence and a leve to lauchen annueles
And take trentales there to to yer to gydere
Serjaunts semed there in selken houes
pleteden for penyes and poundes the lawe
And for love of oure lord un lose here lippes ones
Thow myghtest beter meten myst on Malverne hilles
Than geten a mom of here mouthe er mony were y schewed
Justices jugged that serjeaunts wolde schewe
Were hit wel were hit wrong here word most stande
For thy lak y nat tho lordis lawes they kepe
And saveth us fro sorwes of synful wrecchis
There preched a pardoner as he prest were
And broughte forth a bulle wt bisshopis seles
And seyde that hym self may asoylen hem alle
Of falsenesse of fastinge of vowes y broken
Lewed men leven hym wel liken his wordis
Comen up knelyng to kyssen ye bulle
Bunged hem on the hed blered here eyen
And raughte wt ye ragman rynges and broches
Thus ye given youre gold glotonye to helpe
And leneth hit thus loseles that in lecherie lybbyth
As were the bisshop and worth bothe eres
His sel scholde nat be sent to deceyve the peple
Baksteres and bocheres and brewsteres manye
Wollen webbesteres and weveres of lynnen
Taylours towkeres and tollares bothe
Mylleres and mynstrales and masones some
Of alle libbynge laboreres lopen forth there
As dikeres and delveres that doth here dedis ylle
And dryveth forth the day wt deux save dame Emme
Al this y say in my slep and sevene sythes more
At the heye hyl in the est here wat hit menes
A lovely lady of lere in lynnen y clothed
Com fro the castel and calde me thenne
And seyde sone slepest thow seest this peple
How besy they ben the body for to plese
They han no ware to the hil that on hey standes
Ne no sped of the dongen in the depe dale

y was a ferd of here face thow ho fayr were
And seyde mercy madame what ys this to mene
The tour wt the tofte quod sche treuthe ys ther inne
And wolde that ye wroughten as his word techeth
For he ys fader of fayth and formed yow alle
Bothe wt fel and wt flesch and yaf yow fyue wittes
To worschepe hym ther wt whyle ye ben here
And therfor he hyghte the erthe to helpe yow vchone
Of wollene of lynnene of liflode at nede
In mesurable manere to make yow at ese
And commaunded of his curteysie in comune thre thynges
Aren none nedeful but tho and nempne hem y thenke
And rekene hem by resoun reherse ye hem after
That on ys vesture fram chele the to saue
And mete at thy mele for myseyse of thy sylf
And drynke whan the dryeth ac do nat out of resoun
That thou worthe the wors whan thow wyrche scholdest
For loth in his lyuedays for lykynge of drynke
Dede by his doughtres that the deuel lyked
For lecherie hym laughte and lay by hem bothe
And al a wyt hit the wyn that wykke dede
Drede delitable drynke thow schalt do the bettre
And mesure ys medicyne thogh thow muche yerne
Hit ys nat al good to the gost that the guth hasteth
Ne lyf lode to the lycam that lef ys the soule
Lef nat thy licam for a lyere hym techeth
That ys the wrechyd werld wolde the bytraye
For the fend and thy flesch folweth togydere
And that seeth thy soule and seyth in thyn herte
A madame mercy quod y me lyketh wel youre wordes
Ac the moneye of this molde that men so faste holdeth
Telleth me to wham that tresor apendeth
Go to the gospel that god sayde hym sylfe
Tho the peple hym aposed wt a peny in the temple
Wher they scholde worschepe ther wt cesar the kynge
And god hasked of hem of wham spak the lettre
And the ymage ylyche that ther inne standes
Cesaris thay seyden we seen wel vchone
Reddite cesari quod god that cesari bifalleth
Et que sunt dei deo or ye don ille
For ryghtfullyche resoun scholde reule yow alle
And kynde wyt be wardeyn youre welthe to kepe
And tutor of youre tresor to take hit yow at nede
For hosebondrye and he holdeth togyderes
Trewthe techeth ye so to wyrche there after

Passus primus

I frayned here fayre for hym that here made
The dongeon in the dale that dredful ys of syghth
What may hit mene madame y be seche.

That ys the kastel of care / ho so cometh thero inne
May banne that he bore was / to body or to soule
Thero inne wonyes a wey / that wrong ys hote
Ant eke fader of falsede / formed hym sylf
Adam ant eue he egged to ylle
Consayled kaym / to kylle ys brother
Iudas he by iaped / wt iues of syluer
Ant sennes on an hellerne / hanged hym after
He ys lettare of loue / lyeth hem alle
That trysteth on ys tresor / tyed as sone
Then haued y wonder in my wyt / wat womo he were
That such wyse wordes of holy wryt schewed
Ant halsoned here on the heye name / her ho thennes yede
Wat that a were / that wyssed me so fayre
Bothe of falsenesse ant fayth / fayne wat y hote
Holy chyrche y am quod sche / thow oughtest me to knowe
Y vnderfong the fyrst / ant thy fayth taughte
Ant broughtest me borwes / my byddyng to holde
Wyl thy lyf lasted / to loue me oure alle
Ant eke to be buxum my byddyng to wyrche
Thenne y courbed on my knees / … cryed here of here grace
Preyed here pitously / to prey for my synnes
Ant to kenne me kyndely on cryst to by leue
That y myghte werchyn ys wylle that wroght me to man.
Teche me to no tresor / but telle me thys ylke
How y may saue my soule / that seint hald y holde
Wan alle tresores ar tryed / quod she trewthe ys the beste.
Y do hit on deus caritas / to deme the sothe.
Hit ys as derworthe a drewerye / as dere god hym sylf
For ho ys trewe of ys tonge / ant telleth no other
Doth the werk therewt / wylneth no man ylle
He ys a god be the gospel / agrounde ant alofte
Ant eke y leke to oure lord / by seint lucus lessoun
Clerkus that knoweth hit / scholde kenne hit aboute
For cristene ant vncristene / claymeth hit ychone
Euery wyght that ys wys / wylneth hit to haue
Kynges ant knyghtes / scholde kepen hit be resoun
Ryden an rappe down / in reaumes a boute
Ant take transgressores / ant teyen hem faste
Tyl trewthe haued y termyned / here trespas to the ende
ffor dauid in hys days / dubbed knyghtes
Dede hem swere on here swerd / to serue trewth euere
That ys profession / that apendeth to knyghtes
Ant nat to faste a fryday / in fyf score wynter
Ant halde wt hym ant wt here / that haschet the trewthe
Ant neuer leue hem for loue / ne for lachynge of syluer
Ant he so passeth thys poynt / ys apostata in the hordre
Cryst kyngge kynges knyghted tene
Cherubyn ant seraphyn / such seuene ant another
Yaf hem myghte in hys mageste / the more hym thoughte

And ouer þe mene maynes / made hem archangeles
Taughte hem thorw the trinite / the treuthe to knowe.
To be buxū at þe. bede. & bad hem nat elles/
Lucifer wt legyounes / lerned hit in heuene.
And was the louelokest of lyghte after oure lord selue/
Til he brak boxumnesse / thorw bost of hem selue
thenne fille he wt þe felawshipe / and fendes by come
out of heuene in to helle / hobeled they faste.
Somme in eyr somme in erthe / somme in helle depe
At lucifer lowest / lyth of hem alle/
For pryde that hym pulte out / þe peyne hath no ende/
And apostata of that place / and pelour of helle
And alle that wyrcheth wt wrong / wenden they scholle
after here deth day / and dwelle wt that schrewe
At tho that wyrchen the word / that holy writ techeth
And endeth as y er sayde / in pfite vertue
mowe be syker that here soule / schal wende to heuene
there treuthe his in trinite / and troneth hem alle
For thy y seyde er / by syghte of thys textes
Whan alle tresores ar tryed / treuthe ys the beste. /
co Lere hit thys lewed men / for lettred hit knoweth
that treuthe his the tresor / tryedest on erthe
I haue no kynde knowyng / but mot ye kenne me bettre
by wat craft in my cors / hit comseth and where
Thow doted daffe qd sche / dulle are thy wittes
hit ys a kynde knowyng that kenneth for to loui / thy god leue than thy selue
To do no dedly synne / deye thow scholdest
ffor thy wytnesseth þe word / wyche thow there after
Thys y trowe be treuthe / ho can teche the bettere
loke thow suffre hym to seye / and senes lere hit after
For loue his the leuest thynk / that oure lord asketh
and eke the plente of pees / preche hit in thyn harpe
There thow art murye at thy mete / yf men bit the yedde
co ffor in kynde knowyng in herte / there comseth a myghte
and that falleth to the fader / that formed vs alle.
loked on vs wt loue / let his sone deye mykeliche
for oure mysdedes / to mende vs alle
and yit wolde hem no wo / that wroughte hym that tene.
but mekelyche wt mouthe / mercy he besoughte
To haue pite on the peple / that peyned hym to dethe
here myghte thow se ensaumples / in hym sylf
one that he was myghtful and meke / and mercy gan graunte
To hem that honge hym heye / and þe herte thorlede/
for thy y rede ye ryche / haueth reuthe on the pore
Thow ye be myghty to mote / beth meke in youre werkes
loketh on hem wt loue alles / thow ye hem knewe
for the same mesures that meten amys
Other elles ye schal be wo the wt / whan ye wende hennes,
Thouȝ ye be trewe of youre tonge / and trewlyche wynne
and be as chast as a childe / and do chyrches make

But yif ye loue lelyche | and leue the pore
of such god as god ou sent | godlyche parte
ye habbeth no more merite | in masse ne in houres
then malkyn of here mayden-hod | that no man desyreth
Iames the gentel | iuggeth by ye bokes
that fayth wt oute the fet | ys febler then nauʒt
and as ded as a dore nayl | but yf dedes folwe
Mony chapelyns aren chaste | at charite ys a weye
aren noen harder then thenne | wen they ben avaunsed
and eke vn kynde to here | and to alle other cristene
Chewath here charite | chyde aftr more
here loue ys likned to a lampe | that no lyght ys inne
Such chastite wt oute charite | worth cheyned in helle
for ye curatours | that kepeth yow clene of youre body
and beth acombred wt coveytyse | ye konne nat come out
so harde haveth auarice | yhasped yow to gyderes
Trewthe tauʒhte nere so | but trecherye of elle
and lereth the lewed men | latter to dele
ffor yis wordes y wryte | in the euangelye
Date & dabitr vob | for y dele yow alle
That ys the lok of loue | that leteth oute grace
To conforte the carful | acombred wt synne
loue ys the lyf leche | that oure lord hasteth
and eke the gate of grace | that goth into heuene
ffor thy seye as y seyde er | by syghte of this tyxt
wen alle tresoures ben tryed | trewthe ys the best
Now haue y told the what trewthe ys | taken in thyn herte
y may no lengr lenge the wyth | now loke the oure lord

Passus Secundus

Yet haue y told yow of trewthe | that no tresor ys bettre
yf ye wyl weten of wronge | y wyl yow fayre schewe
Bothe of fauel and falsede | that myche folk apeyreth
ffor yut y kneled on my knees | and cryed here of grace
and seyde mercy madame | for marie loue of heuene
that bar that blysful barn | that boughte us on the rode
kenne me for youre cortesye | the false for to knowe
loke on the lyft half qd sche | and lo were a staunde
bothe fauel and falsse | and ye feres monye
Yf thow wylnes to wyte | lo were they wende
y loked on my lifthalf | as the lady me taughte
and was ware of a womman | worthelyche y clothed
ypurfyled in pelure | the best on erthe
ycorouned in a corone | the kyng hath no better
alle here fyue fyngres were floured wt ryngs
wt ryche rubies | as rede as a glede
in red scarlet y robed | and rybanes of golde
there ys no quene queyntere | that quyk ys on molde
wat ys that womman qd y | so worthyly atyred
that ys mede the mayde qd he | hath noyed me ful ofte

wat ys that womman

And lakked my lore to lordes aboute
In the popes paleys he ys pryue as my-selue
And so scholde sche nat be for wrong ys here syre
Out of wrong sche wax to wroth hele monye
I howghte ben herer than he y com of a bettre
To morwe worth the mariage mad of mede & of fals
Fauel with fayr speche hath forged hem to-gederes
And gyle hath by-gete here so he graunteth alle he wylle
Ac alle ys lyares ledyng that they lye to-gederes
To morwe worth the mariage y mad as y telle
There myghte thow wyte yf þu wylt whyche thay ben alle
That longeth to thys lordschipe the lasse & the more
Knowe hem there if thow canst and kepe the fro hem alle
yf thow wylnest to wone with treuthe in ys blisse
Y may no lenger lette lord y the by-kenne
And by-come a good man for eny coueytyse y rede
Alle the ryche retenaunce that regneth with false
Were bede to this brydale on bothe to the sydes
Syre Symonye ys of sent to sele the chartres
And alle the notaryes by name that they nere fayle
To sette on here sygnes as Symonye wyl bydde
Cyuyle ys comaunded to sese alle the londes
That fauel and fals by eny fyn haldeth
To feffe mede there-myd in mariage for euere
Sothnesse and my-self sey this and more
For there nas hale ne howse to herborwe the peple
Nayther legge ne lawende ne lesewe so brode
That ech feeld nas ful of folk alle aboute
In myddys on morwe on a mountayne here
Was pyght vp a pauelon proud for the nones
An ten thowsande of tentes telde by sydes
Of knyghtes of contrays and comuneres aboute
For sysores for somnours for sellares and byggares
For lered for lewed for laborers in thorpes
Alle to wytnesse wel what the wryt wolde
In what manere that mede in mebles was sesed
And to be fastened with fals the fyn ys a rered
Thenne fauel fecheth here forth and to fals taketh
In forward that falsed schal fynde hure for euer
And to be bonn at ys bede at bord and at bedde
As syre Symonye wyl segge to sewen ys wylle
Symonye and Cyuyle thenne stondeth forth
And vnfoldeth the feffement that fals hath y-maked
Thus by-gynneth these gomes and gredeth ful here
Sychet and wytnesseth that woneth on erthe
That y fauel feffe falsenesse to mede
To be prynses of pryde an pore and in ryche
With alle the lordschepe of lecherye a lengthe and of brede
Wyth the erldom of enuye for euere to laste
And alle the counte of coueytyse y knowen aboute

As in chirche in chapitre in other chevalrie
Tyl that glotenye be y grave here glorye to derye
Wt the seyneworye of clerkche y sese hem to gydere
Then to habbe and to holde and here heyres after
Wt alle the pertenaunce of purgatorie in to the pyne of helle
yeldyng for this thyng at one yeres ende
here soules to Satanas to synken in pyne
there to wonyen wt wrong while god ys in heuene
In wytnesse of wych thyng wrong was the furste
and Peres the pardoner of seint poules chirche
and Dauid the bedel of bokyngham schire
and Reynald the reue of rotelonde sokene
Monde the mylnare and mony mo other
In the date of deuil this dede ys a seled
By syght of syre Symonye and Syuyles leue
Thenne tened hym theologye when he this tale y herde
and seyde to Syuyle now sorwe on thy bokes
Such weddyng to wirche to wrathe the treuthe
and ar this weddyng be wrought wo the be tyde
For Mede ys moylere of Mendes engendret
god graunteth hym sylf to gyue Mede to treuthe
and thow hast gyue here to a glotoun now god gyue the sorwe
the tyxt telleth nat so treuthe wot the sothe
Dignus est operarius his huyre to haue
and thow hast faste here wt false wo fy on thi lawe
for alle by lesynges thow lyuest and lecherous werkes
thow schalt a buggen this bargayn by my fader sowle
Syre Symonye and thy syluen schendeth holy chirche
Wt notaryes nysottes myrest the peple
and soulest yow in synne wt seinte marye preiere
Wel ye wyte wernardes but yf youre wyt fayle
That fals hys a faytor and faytles of werkes
and as a bastard y bore of belsabubbes kynne
and Mede ys a mayde mulyerist on erthe
a mighte kysse the kyng for cosyn and he wolde
As wircheth by wysdom and by wyt after
and ledeth here to londone there lawe hys handled
yf any lawe wyl loke they lygge to gyderes
and thow iustices iugged here to be ioyned wt false
yit beth y war of the weddyng for wytty hys treuthe
For conscience ys of ys consayl and knoweth yow echon
and yf he fynde yow in defaute and wyt the fals holde
hyt schal be sytte youre sowle ful sowre at the laste
here to assentede Syuyle ac Symonye ne wolde
Tyl he hadde syluer for hys seles and signes to gyderes
Thenne fette fauel forth floryns y nowe and bad gyle golde alle a boute
To Symonye and Syuyle and sethe alle the other
and namelyche the notaryes that there non fayle
and feffe false wytnesse wt floryns y nowe
For he may mede a maystrye and make at my wylle

Tho this gold was ygyue / gret was the thonkyng
To fals and to Fauel / for here faire yftes
And come to conforte / fram care the false
And seiden certes sire / cese schal we neuer
Til mede be thy wedded wyf / thorw wit of vs alle
We han mede amaystred / thorw oure mery speche
That he hath graunted to go / with a god wylle
To londone to loke / yf that lawe wolde
Jugge yow ioyntely / in ioye to gyderes
Thenne was falsenesse fayn / and Fauel as blythe
And lete sompne al the segges / in schyres abowte
And bad hem alle be bown / beggares and other
To wenden with hym to westmynstre / to wytnesse this dede
Thenne kared they for caples / to carye hem thedir
Ac Fauel bad feche forth / foles ynowe
And sette mede on a scherreue / yschoed al newe
And fals on a sysour / that softeliche trotted
And Fauel on fayr speche / feyntliche atyred
Thenne haued notaries none / annoyed they were
For symonye and Cyuile / scholden gon on here fete
Thenne swor Cyuile / and seyde by the rode
That somponoures scholde be sadeled / and serue symonye
And lat aparayle the prisoneres / in palfrayes wyse
Sire symonye hym self / schal sytte on here bakkes
For deenes schulle ben dyght as destreres
They schal bere thes bysshopes / til they be there
Erchedekenes officiales / y hote that they ben atyred
For they schul serue my self / that Cyuile hatte
And lat cartsadele the commessarie / oure cart schal he drawe
And fetten oure vitayles of fornicatores
And maketh lyare a lankayt / to lede alle thys other
As fobbes and faytoures / that on here fet rennes
Thenne fals fareth forth and Fauel to gyderes
And mede in the myddel / and alle thys men after
I haue no tome to telle / the tayl that hem folwed
Of many maner men / that on thys molde libbes
Ac gyle was forgong / and gyded hem to lede
Ac sothnesse sey hym wel / seyde but lyte
Ac fiched hym faste / and goth afore alle
And com to the kynges court / and conscience tolde
And conscience to the kyng / carped it after
And how thys cursed companie / that to the court wolde
Of symonye of Cyuile / and seyde hym al to gyderes
How Fauel and falsenesse / fonded to lacche mede
To mariage and on wat maner hym lette
And how gyle gaf the gold / to gomes abowte
To symonye to Cyuile and seyde al to gyderes
And how teologye tened hym / and traytoures hem called
And seyde trewthe for here trespas / scholde tene hem ych one
Bi crist quod the kyng tho / and y cacche myghte

Fals other fauel/or eny of here feres
y wyl be wreke of tho wrecchys/that wyrche so ylle
and do hange hem by the hals/and alle that hem menteynneth
Schal neuer man on this molde/menprise the leste
But ryght as lawe loketh/lat fal on hem alle
ffor eny syluer of mede/by marye of heuene
and commaunded a constable/that com at the furste
To atache tho tyrauntes/for eny tresor y hote
Fetereth falsenesse faste/for eny skynes yftes
and gurdeth of gyles heued/lat hym go no forther
and bryngeth mede to me/maugre hem alle
Symonye and cyuyl/y sende hem to warne
That holy chyrche for hem/worth harmed for euere
and thow lacche lyare/lat hym nat ascape
Tyl he be put on the pylory/for eny preyere y hote
Drede at the dore stod/and the dome herde
How the kyng constables/commaunded and other
as seriauntes and scheryues/that schyres han to kepe
Wayned fals forth/and ys feres alle
Thenne falsenesse for fere/fley to the freres
Gyle doth hym to/a gast for to dye
Ac marchauntes mette with hym/made hym abyde
By schetten hym in here schoppe/to schewen here ware
Parled hym as a prentys the peple to serue
Lyghtlyche lyare/lep away thenne
Lurkynge thorw lanes/to lugged of mony
He was nawhar welcome/for ys mony tales
But ouer al y houted/and y hote trusse
Tyl pardoneres haued pyte/pulled hym in to howse
Wosche and wyped hym/wonden hym in clothes
And sente hym on sonday with seles to chyrches
and gaf pardoun for pans/pound mele aboute
Thenne lowred leches/and letres they hym sent
ffor to wonye with hem/waters to loke
Spiceres speke to hym/to spyen here thyng
ffor he cowthe of here craft/and knew mony gummes
Ac mynstrales and messageres/mette with hym ones
and helden hym half yer/and eleue dayes
ffreres with fayre speche/fette hym thennes
ffor knowyng of comeres/coped hym as a frere
Ac he hath leue to lepe out/as ofte as hym lyketh
and ys welcome when a wol/woneth with hem ofte
Alle fledde for fere/saue fauel and mede
Ac bothe to trembled/attached tho they were

Passus tercius

Now ys mede the mayde and no mo of hem alle
With bedeles and bayles y brought to the kyng
The kyng calde a clerk y can nat ys name
To take mede the mayde and maken here at ese

y schal assay here my sylf and sothelyche apose
wat man of thys world that here were leuest
and yf he wyrche by wyt and my wille folwe
y wille fo(r)gyue here that gult so me god helpe
Corteyslyche thys clerk as the kyng hyghte
ladde this lady to lofte that mede his y hote
at there was myrthe and mynstracie mede to plese
That woneth at Westmenstre worscheped here alle
Gentelyche wt ioye the iustises monye
Busked hem to the bour there the burde dwelde
Conforted here kyndelyche by clergys leue
Seyden mourne nat mede ne mak thow no sorwe
For we wyl wysse the kyng and thy way schape
For to wedde at thy wille were thow lef lyketh
For al consciences cast and craft as we trowe
Myldelyche mede mercyed hem alle
Of theyr grete goodnesse and gaf hem vchone
Coupes of clene gold coupes of syluer
Rynges wt rubyes and rychesses monye
The leste man of here meyne a mote of golde
Thenne laughte they leue this lordes at mede
Wt that come clerkes conforted here the same
and beden here be blythe for we beth thyn owne
For to wyrche thy wille wyle thow myzt loke
Hendelyche he thenne by hyghte hem the same
To loue yow lelely wyle my lyf dureth
and in the consistorye at court do calle youre name
and bygge benefices were yow best lyketh
Porchase prebendes there to wyle my pane lasteth
Schal no lewednesse lette hem that y louye
That they nat first avaunsed for y am y knowe
There connynge clerkes cloketh by hynde
The kyng fro counsayl com called after mede
and of sentaste as swythe seriauntes here fette
and broughte here to boure wt a blythe chere
Corteyslyche the kyng commesed to telle
To mede the mayde meued his wordes
Vnwyttyly thow womman wrowte hast ofte
ac worse wrowghtest nere as when yow fals toke
ac y forgyue that gult and graunte the grace
and fro hennes to thy deth day do yow so no more
J haue a knyzt conscience com late fro by yende
yf he wylneth the to wyue wolte yow hym haue
ye lord qd that lady lord hit me forbede
but y be holy at youre heste lat hange me ellis
Thenne was conscience y cald to come and apere
by fore the kyng and ye counsayl of clerkes and other
Knelede conscience and to the kyng lowted
and what that ye wille were and what he do scholde
Wylt yow wedde thys lady and y wyl assente

for he ys fayn of thy fellawschippe and for to be thy make
Nay quod conscience to the kyng crist hit me for bede
Er y wedde such a wyf wo me by tyde
Sche ys frele of here fayth fikel of here speche
a maketh men mys do many score tyme
In tryste of here tresor he teneth ful monye
Wyues and wedewes wantownesse he techeth
lereth hem lecherye that loueyeth here yftes
youre fader a felde thorw false by heste
poysened popes apeyreth holy chirche
ys nat a bettere bawde by hym that me made
by twene heuene and helle and erthe thow me sowte
Sche ys tykel of here tayl tale wys of tonge
as comoun as the cart way to knaues and to alle
to monekes to mynstrales to meseles in hegges
Sysoures and sompnoures such men here preyseth
a doth men lesen here land ya and here lyf bothe
Schereues of schyres were schent yf he nere
ffor he lat passe prysoneres payeth for hem ofte
a gyueth the gaylares gold and grotes to gyderes
To vnfetere the fals fle were hym lyk
Taketh trewthe by the top teyeth hym faste
And hangeth hym for hatrede that harmed neuere
To be cursed in the consistorye a counteth nat a rysch
for a copeth the comyssarye coteth ys clerkes
Sche ys assoyled as sone as here self lyketh
he may ney as myche do in a monthe ones
as youre secrete sel in syxe score dayes
ffor he ys pryue wt the pope prouisores hit knoweth
ffor symonye and here self a seleth here bulles
a blesseth thes bysschopes thow they be lewede
Prouendereth persones prestes he meynteneth
To habbe lemmanes and lotebys all here lyf dayes
and bryngeth forth barnes a yeyn forbode lawes
Where he ys wel wt a kyng wo ys the rewme
ffor he ys fauorable to fals and falleth ryght ofte
Barones and burgeyes he bryngeth in to sorwe
By ihc wt here iueles youre iustyses a schendeth
And lyth a yeyn lawe and letteth hem the gate
that faith may nat haue ys forth here floreynes goth so thykke
The mase for a mene man thowz a mote euere
Wt oute gyfte or mede. or margage ys lawe
lawe ys so lordlyche and loth to make ende
Wt. oute presentes or pans a pleseth ful fewe
he lat lawe as here lust and louedayes maketh
Clergyse and coueytyse he coupleth to gyderes
Thys ys the lyf of that lady now lord yf here sorwe
and alle that meynteneth here men meschaunce hem by tyde
for pore men han no power to pleyne hem they hem smerte
Such a mayster ys mede a monges men of gode

Thanne morned mede mened here to the kyng
To haue space to speke spede yf a myghte
The kyng graunted here grace wt a god wylle
Excuse yf thow canst y can no more schewen
For consciens acusseth to congey the for euer
Nay lord quath that lady leue hym the worse
Whan the wyte wytly where the wrong lyges
There that meschef ys gret mede may helpe
And thow knowest consciens y com nat to chyde
Ne to depraue thy persone wt a proud herte
Wel thow wost werne but yf tow wyl gabbe
Thow hast hanged on myn half elleuene tymes
And eke y grype my gold gef hit where thow lyked
As wy thow wrathestu the now wonder me thynketh
For yut y may as y myghte meske the wt yftes
And multiplye thy manhede more thanne thow knowest
Ac thow hast defamed me foule a for the kyng here
That thow seydest for soth schalt thow nere fynde
For me were leuere by oure lord to lygge in peyne
Wyle that thys world last the wyche so ylle
For kyld y nere no kyng ne conseylled there after
Ne dede as thow demyst y do yt on the kynge
In normandye was a nat a noyed for my sake
Ac thow thy self sothelyche schamedest ofte
Crope in to kaban for cold of thy nayles
Wendest that wynter wolde last euere
Dradyst the to dey for a dymme cloude
And hastedest hamward for hunger of thy wombe
Wt oute pyte thow pyte thow pylor pore men
Thow robbedest and bere here bras at thy bak to kaleys to sylle
There y lefte wt my lord ys lyf for to saue
And made ys men myrye and mournyng to leue
Y battered hem on the bak bolded here hertes
Dede hem hoppe for hope to haue me at wylle
Haued y be marchal of ys men by mary of heuene
Y durst haue leyd my lyf and no lasse wedde
A scholde haue be ~~kyng~~ lord of that lond a lengthe and of brede
And eke kyng of that kyth ys kyn for to helpe
Ye the leste brol of ys blod a barones pere
Cowardlyche thow consciens conseylest hym thennes
To leuen ys lordschepe for a lytel sylner
That ys the rychest reaume that reyn ouer houes
Ac consciens cyst wot as y can descryue
Out of northfolk or normandye thy name was y founde
For thow canst selle the dowh y alse and wt oute
Halse wt hym and wt here ay as the lauth
Freres fyndeth the a fferm that thow fyrst blamedest
Thy selue art a sentaunte that they schal me schryue
Fyrst thow come hem a cope consciens thy selue
And camalbuedest yche comen conceytyse to lere

ant nyme nat of no man but as nede hastheth
Now ar thow coped hem in coueytyse ant counseth to yrde
What weren wones to wade in wynteres ful colde
Now beth they boted tho bewsonn ant bayayn crowlyche be scrypeth
The bonghokest bornet ant blanket to selle
They byggen hyt nat begge hit to bakke there nime
In delys of lecherye ys lyeam a chorch
That such wedes wereth y wyl yt a wolde
For lecherye ys delyt ant eke a lost bothe
leyed ant vnleyed lewdelyche thow techest
vnnethe ys ther eny man that nolde be ryche
Ant alle the wytes that abot to wynnygge he schapeth
Of alle maner men mede ys desyred
Consciense but at consayl comitheth ful selde
Marthamis myghte for here the nono man berere
Consciense in coueytyse clepeth yobes
Ant coyleth men for synnes we sen wel oure synne
Consciense ys the comsyng of alle synnes werst
he hyt wel be hit wo a wot hyt at the furst
ys maystry ys a bone no that mede any bere
w^t oute hys wyt wych y not god wot the sothe
That thow ne art furst founde godfayth ne knoweth

Passus quartus

Cesseth cesseth sayde the kynge y soffre yow no lenger
ye schal saghtene for sothe ant serue me bothe
Kysse he ys the kyngs consciense y hote
Nay by cryst ys consciense congeye me arst
Ant resoun rade me ther tyl rather wylly deye
Ant y comawnde ys the kyngs to consciense thenne
rape the to ryde ant resoun that thow feche
Comawnde hym that he come my consayl to here
For he schal rewle my reame rede me the beste
Of mede ant me oth^er ant what man schal here wedde
Ant acounte w^t the consyence so me cryst helpe
how thow lerest the peple lered ant lewed
y am fayn of y forward seyth the freke thenne
Ant ryt ryght to resoun ant rowneth in ys ere
seyde hym as the kyngs seide ant sethe tok ys leue
I schal a raye me to ryde qd resoun reste the the wil
Ant calde tomme trewe tonge telle me no tale
no lesyngs to lawhe of for y loued hit neuere
Sette my sadel vp on suffre tyl y se my tyme
Ant lat warroke wyl wyth stronge wytty gyrthes
honge on hym the heuye brydel to holde ys hened lowe
For yit wyl he make mony a wehe ar we be there
Thenne consyence on ys capel caryes forth faste
Ant resoun ryt forth w^t hym ryght to the kyng
As on waryn wysdom ant witty ys fere

folwed hem faste for they haued to done
In the cheker and in chauncerye to be descharged of thing
and ryde faste for resoun schold rede hem the beste
ffor to saue hem sylf fro schame and fro harmes
Ac constience com arst to court by a myle
and romed forth wt resoun ryght to the kyng
Curteysliche the kyng com a ye resoun
and by twene hym sylf and ys sone sette hym a benche
and worden ful wysly a gret wyle to gyderes
Thenne com pes in the plement and potte vp a bille
hou wronge a yeyne ys wylle haued ys wyf take
and hou a rauesched rose reynaldes loue
and margrete of here maydenhod maugre here chek
Bothe my ges and my grys ys gadelynges fecheth
y dar nat for fere of hym fyghte ne chyde
a borwed of me bayard and broughte a yeyn nere
ne no ferthyng there fore for nought y couthe plede
a meyntayneth ys men to morther myn hewes
fforstalleth my fayres fyghteth in my chepyng
Breketh vp my bern dore bereth a wey my whete
Taketh me but a tayle for ten quarter otes
and yut a bet me there to lyth by my mayde
y am nat hardy for hym vnnethe to loke
The kyng knewe he seyde sothe for consyence hym tolde
and sothenesse also hit was sothe that he tolde
and thenne was wronge wo and wysdom a soughte
To make ys pays wt ys pans and profred hym monye
and seyde hadde y loue of my lord litel wold y rech
Thow pes and ys power pleynen hem euere
Wysdom wan tho and so dede wyt also
ffor that wrong haued y wroughte so wyked a dede
and warned wrong tho wt such a wys tale
he so wyrcheth be wyl wrathe maketh ofte
y sey by thy sylf thow schalt hyt sone fynde
but yf mede hit make thy meschef ys vppe
Bothe thy lyf and thy lond lyth in ys grace
Wrong thenne on wysdom wepes faste
to kepe hym for his handy dandy payed
Thenne wysdom and wyt wenten to gyderes
an nome mede myd hem mercy to wynne
Pes potte forth ys heued an his panne blody
wt oute gilt god wot gat y this scathe
Consience and the kyng knewe wel the sothe
and wysten wel that wrong was a schrewe euer
Ac wysdom and wyt were a boute faste
To ouercome the kyng thorw catel if they myghte
The kyng swor by Cryst and by ys crowne bothe
That wrong for ys werk schold wo tholie
and comaunded a constable to caste hym in yrenes
a schal nat this vij yer y se ys fete ones

God wot ȝe wysdom that were nat the beste
ant he amendes mowe make lat meynprise hym haue
ant be borw for ye bale begge hym mercy
Amende that a mysdede ant euere more the bettre
Wyt acorded the wyth ant seyde the same
Bet ye that bote bale adoun brynge
Then bale be ybete ant bote neuer the bettre
Thenne gan mede to meke here ant mercy besowte
ant profered pees a present al of pure gold
ant seyde haue this of me to amende thy scathe
For y wyl wage for wronge he wyl do so no more
Pytensliche pees thenne preyed the kynge
to haue mercy on that mysdede hym ofte
For he hath waged me wel as wysdom hym taughte
y forgyue hym that gult wt a good wylle
So that ye assente y can sey no more
For mede hath made my mendes y may no more aske
Nay quod the kynge tho so god yf me blysse
Wronge wendes nat so away er y wyte more
Lope he so lyghtly away lawen he wolde
ant eft the balder to be to bete myn hewes
But resoun haue rewthe on hym he schal reste hym in my stokes
As longe as y leue but the more loue hit make
Summe radden resoun to haue rewthe on the schrewe
ant to counsayle the kynge for conscience sake
that mede moste be meynpernor resoun they besowte
Rede me nat quod resoun no rewthe to haue
tyl lordes ant ladyes louye in trewthe
ant purnele purfil be putte in here whiche
Tyl childrene cherysynge ben chasted wt yerdes
ant harlotes holynesse y holde for an hyne
Tyl clerkes ant knyȝtes be corteys of here mowthes
ant hatyn harlotrye to here yt or to mowthe hit
Tyl prestes here prechynge preue hit on hem sylf
ant do hit in dede to drawen vs to gode
Tyl seynt James be sought there y schal assygne
That no man go to galys but yf he go for euere
ant alle rome renneres for robberes of by ȝende
Be here no syluer ouer see that sygne of kynge schewith
Nayther grotes ne gold ygraue wt kynges corone
vp forfeture of that fe he so fynt hym at douere
But yf he marchaunt be or his man or messager wt lettres
Or prest or prysoner that the pope ~~auaunceth~~ auaunceth
Thenne schal y knele to the kynge ant crien hym of grace
For wronges werkes ant wrathe in hope that he amende
In none manere elles nat for no maner bysechynges
Waren wysdom ant wytty his fere
Cowthe nat wappe a word tho to wt segge resoun
But stoden stylle as stany hors that dolleth
Conscience ant the kynge acorded to resoun

And seyden that resoun ryghtfullyche haued schewed
Ac ys hit ful hard by myn heued her to to brynge hit
Alle my lege lede to lede hem thus euene
By hym that raughte on the rode quod resoun to the kyng
But yf thow rewle thi rewme resoun schal nere
Thow schalt rewle my rewme resoun and ryde by my syde
Nay redyly quod resoun y schal no ryght schewe
Wyle mede hat the maystrye to mote in thys halle
Ac y schal schewe ensamples as y se othe
Ac y sey for my sylf and hit so be folle
That y were kynge wt crowne to kepen a rewme
Schulde neuer wrong in thys world that y wyte myzte
Be vnpunysched in my power for perel of my soule
Ne gete my grace thorw gyfte so me god helpe
Ne for no mede haue mercy but mekenesse hit make
For nullum malum the man mette wt inpunitum
& nullum bonum the bolde be irremuneratum
Lat thy confessour syre kyng construe the thys englis
And yf ye wyrcheth in dede y wedde myn eres
That lawe schal be a laborer and lede a felde donge
And loue schal lede the as the lef lyketh
Clerkes that were confessoures coupled hem to gyderes
For to construe thys clause declined faste
Ac to resoun among the rynkes haued y rehersed this wordes
Ther nas man in the mote more ne lasse
That ne held mekenesse a mayster and mede a muche wrech
And Waren be seynt rycher a schent the rewme
Loue let of here lyte lawghed here to scorne
And seyde so loudde that sothnesse hit herde
Ho so wylneth here to wyue for welth of here goodes
But he be cokewold ykald kutte of my nose
Consyence quyk wot knewe wel the sothe
The kyng and resoun a ryse and ryden in to chambre
And busked to bowe y be held hem no lenger

Passus quintus

Wayeyn wysdom and Wytty ys fere
Cowthe nat wappen a word to wt segge resoun
But staared for studying as a ston stylle
The kyng a corded by crist to resoun sawes
And seyde that resoun ryghtfullyche haued schewed
Ac hit ys ful hard by myn heued her to to brynge hit
And my lege lede to lede thus euene
By hym that raughte on the rode quod resoun to the kyng
But y rewle thus thy rewme rend of my heres
yf ye bydde buxumnesse be of myn assente
And y assente quod the kyng by seynt mary my lady
Be my counsayl y come of clerkes and herles
Ac redyly resoun thow schalt nat ryde hennes
For as longe as y lyue leue y the nelle.

J. am. a. redy qd reson to reste wt yow euere
So consyence be of oure consayl kepe y no bettere
And y graunte qd the kyng goddes forbode he fayle
As longe as y lyue libbe we togederes
The kyng and ys knyȝtes to the kyrke wente
To here matynes and masse and to the mete after
Thenne wakede y of my wynkyng and wo was wt alle
That y ne hadde slepe sadder and y seyn more
Ar y hadde fare a forlong feyntise me hent
That y ne myȝte forther a fot for slep that me folwed
y sat softely a doun sayde by my leue
And so y bablede on my bedes they brouȝte me a slepe
And say muche more then fore telle
For y saw the feld ful of folk that y a fore tolde
And consience wt a cros com for to preche
And preyde the peple haue pyte of hem sulue
And preued the pestilence was for pure synne
And southe westerne wynd a saterday at eue
Was pertliche for pruyde and for no poynt elles
For word ye but wynd and so my wyt telleth
As wel y wot that holy wryt wot muche bettere
And wytnesseth that goddes word ye worthyeste of alle
Hit maketh the messe and the masse that men vnderfongeth
For goddes body and ye blod bryngeth to saue
Helle yates hit to braste and hadde out Adam
Wt wynd of ye word al this world made
And in ensaumple segges that ye schal do the bettere
Beches and brod okes weren blowe to the erthe
Al to warne ye wyse what thys were menes
Peres and plomtres were poste to the erthe
Asshes and helmes and okes ful heye
Turne vpward here tayl yn tokyng of drede
That dedly synne ar domesday for do schal hem alle
Of thys matere y myȝte mamele ful longe
Ac y schal seye as y say so me god helpe
How consyence wt ye cros cumseth to preche
A bad waster to wyrche what a beste couthe
To wynne here wastyng wt somme manere craft
And preyde pernele here porfil to leue
To kepe hit in here cofre consyence by solde
~~Thomme~~ Thomme stowe a taȝte to take to staues
And fette hom felice from wyue pyne
Warned wat ye wyf was to blame
That here heued was at alf mark and ye hode at a grote
A bad bette to kytte a bowȝ or tweye
And bete beton there myde but yf he wolde wyrche
Chargede chapmen to chaste here chyldren
Let no wynnyng forwanyen hem whyle they ben yonge
preyede prelates and prestes y fere that they prechyde the peple
preue hit in hem sylf and libbe as they lere vs we wol leue hem the bettere

And seide a parde religioun here rewle to holde
Lest the kyng and his counsayl youre comunes apeyre
And be stywardes of youre stedes til ye be stywed bettere
And ye that seken seyn James and seyntes of Rome
Ihū and ierres and Iacobes welle
Seken seynt trewthe for he may saue you alle
Qui cū patre & filio that fayre hem byfalle
That seth as y seie wyle here dayes lasten
The sone wt the seynt spirit saue he fro meschaunce
That seketh my sarmo and thus seith trewthe
Thanne ran repentaunce reherssed his teme
And gerte wylle to wepe wat wt his eyes
Pernele proude herte platte here to the erthe
And lay longe er a loked and lord mercy cryed
And by hyghte to hym that us alle made
A scholde vn sowen here serk and sette there an hayre
For to afayten here flessh that fers was to synne
Schal neuere heye herte me hente but holde me lowe
And suffre to be mys seyd and so dide y neuere
But now wyl y meke me and mercy byseche
Of alle hem that y haue had envye in myn herte
Lechoure seyde alas and oure lady cryed
To make mercy for his mysdedes bytwene god and his soule
Wt a scholde this saterday seuen yer ther aft
Drynke but wt the doke and dyne but ones
Enuye and yre . ayther wep faste
Preyede furst to pouert and tho peny alse
To gete gree for here gilt of god that hem boughte
That neuere wyked wylle ne wrath hem ouere come
But sende hem grace to suffre and synne to lete
And for to louye and to be loued as charite wolde
Thenne com coueityse knoked his brest.
A hauede a northfolke nose y noem til god here
And swor by so thenk that synne scholde he lete
And neuere wolle to wey no worstedes make
No morgage maner wt moneye that he hauede
But wenden to walsynghm and my wyf alse
And bydde the rode of bromholm brynge us out of dette
Thenne gan glotoun to grete and gret sorwe made
Al for his lytherlyf that a lyued hadde.
And a vowed faste . for eny hungr or thurste
Schal neuere fysch up on the fryday defye in my wombe
Ar abstinence myn aunte haue yf me leue
And yut hath he hated me al my lyf tyme
Slewthe for sorwe fil down . y swowe
Tyl vigilate and veyles fette wat at his eyl
Flatted hit on his face and faste on hym cryed
And seyde war the fro wanhope . wolde the to trayse
Ych am sory of my synnes sey to thy selue
And bete thy sylf on thy brest bydde hym of grace

For his no gult here so ~~gay~~ gret that his goodnesse ne his more
Thenne sat Sleuthe up . seynede hym faste
ant made . a vow to fore god for ys foule synne
Schal no sonenday be this seuen yer but syknesse yt make
that . y . ne schal do me ar day to the dere chyrche
To here masse ant matynes as . y . a monek were
Schal none alle aft^er^ mete halde me thennes
Tyl y haue euensong . y . herd . y . by . hote wyle . y . lybbe
And yet y wil yelde ayeyn yf . y so myche haue
Al that . y . wykedly wan . senes . y . wyt hadde
Thowz my lyflode lake leten . y . nelle
Than ych man schal haue hys ar . y . hennes wende
ant wt . the residue ant the remenaunt
By the rode of chestre seke seynt treuthe ther wt . or . y . se rome
or james or jerusalem by ihc of heuene .
Robert the robbere on reddite lokede
Ac for he hadde nat were wt . a wep ful sleythe sore
Ac yut the synful schrewe seyde to hym sylue
Cryst that up . on . caluary up on the cros deydest
Tho dismas my brother by soughte of grace
ant hauedest mercy for his mysdedes for memento ones
So rewe on me robert that reddere ne habbe
ne neuer wene to wynne wt craft that . y knowe
Thy wille worth up on me as . y wel disserue
To haue helle for euere nere hope . a . that . y . haue
for youre muchyl mercy mytygacion . y . by seche
for sothe no vale so feble ar my bones
Caucyon ant . y . couthe caute wolde . y make
That . y . ne begged ne borwed ne in despeyr deyde
Ac what byfel of this felown . y . can nat fayre schewe
Wel . y . wot a wep faste water wt ys eyes
ant knowleched ys coupe yut est sones to cryst
that penitencia ys pyk . a . wolde polsche newe
ant lepe wt hym ouer lond al ys lyf dayes
for that he lay by latro lucifers aunte
A thowsend of men tho throngen to gydyres
Wepyng ant waylyng for here mysdedes
Cryende upward to cryst an to ys clene moder
grace to go to treuthe god leue that . a . mote
Ac there was weye so wys ~~there~~ that the way thyder couthe
But blostred forth as bestes ouer baches ant hilles
Tyl late ant longe that they . a . lede mette
y payled as . a . paynym in palmeres wyse
A bar . a . bordoun . y . bounde wt . a . brode lyste
In . a . wethewyse . y . wownden . a . boute
A . bagge ant . a . bolle he bar by ys syde
an hundret of hampulles on ys hatte sete
Sygnes of syse ant schelles of galis
ant many . a . crowche on ys clok ant keyes of rome
ant the vernycle . a . fore for men scholde . y . knowe & se be ys signes wham
. a . sowght adde

Passus Sextus

This folk frayned hym first fro whennes a come
Fram synay a sayde and fro the sepulcre of oure lorde
Bedlehem and babelonye y haue y sought bothe
In Ermonye in alisaundre in many oth^r places
ye mowe se by my sygnes that sitteth on my hatte
That y haue walked ful wyde in wete and in drye
And soughte gode seyntes for my sowle hele
Ac knowest thow ought a corseynt that men calleth treuthe
Cowthest wissen us the way there that wye dwelleth
Nay so me god helpe seyth the gome thenne
y say neuere palmere with pyk ne with scrippe
Axen aft^r hym er now in this place
Pet^r quod a plowman and putte forth his heued
y knowe hym as kyndely as clerk doth ys bok
Conscyence kenede me to his place
And sennes y suryed hym to serue hym for euere
Bothe to sowe and to sette whyle y swynke myghte
I haue ben ys folwere al this fourty wynter
Bothe y sowen ys seed sewed his bestes
And eke y kept ys corn y carryed hit to howse
y dyked and y dolue do that a highte
Bothe with inne and with oute y wayted ys profit
There ys no laborer in this lordschepe that a loueth bettre
For thow y sey hit my self y serue hym to paye
y haue myn huyre of hym wel and oth^r whyle more
He ys the prestest payere that pore men y knoweth
He with halt non hewe ys huyre that he ne hath hit at eue
He ys as low as a lomb and louelich of speche
yf ye wilneth to wyte were this wye dwelleth
y schal wisse yow the way wel ryght to ys place
ye leue peres quod the pilegrimes and profred hym huyre
Nay quod perkin the plowman by the peril of my sowle
I nolde nat fonge a ferthyng for seint thomas schryne
Treuthe wold loue me the wers a long tyme aft^r
Ac ye wilne to wende this ys the wey thedre
ye mote go thorw mekenesse bothe man and wyues
Tyl come in to consyence crist wot the sothe
That loueth hym leuere than your^e owne hertes
And your^e neyheboros next in none wyse apeyre
oth^r wyse than thow wost a wroughte to thy self
And so boweth by a brok beth buxum ys called
For to ye fynden a ford youre faderes anhoureth
Wadeth in at that water and wassche yow wel there
And ye schal lyue the leng^r by a long tyme
So schalt thow se swere nat but yf hit be for nede
And namlyche an ydel the name of oure lorde
And holde so tho alway heye tyl ende
Thenne schalt yow come by a croft but come yow nat ther inne
The croft hatteth coueyte nat mennes catel ne wyues
Brek nat a bow ther of but yf hit be thyn owne

To stokkes there standeth at steinte yow nat there
They hatte Stele nat ne Sle nat strik forth by bothe
lef hem on thy lift hond and loke nat there aftir
Thenne schalt thow blenche at a berow bere no false witnesse
ys frethyd in wt floreynes and other fees monye
ploke thow plonte there for pel of thy soule
Thenne schalt thow se seysoth so it be to done
at in no manere elles nat for no mannes byddyng
Thenne schalt yow come to a court as clere as the sonne
The mote ys of mercy the maner a boute
and alle the walles of wyt to holde wel thyroute
The carneles ben of confort cristene to saue
and botrased wt byleuyng to brynge me to heuen
Alle the hous ben y heled halles and chambres
wt no led but wt loue that longeth to the place
The toure there trewthe ys hym self ys vp to the sonne
a doth wt the day sterre that hym dere liketh
a may do in the mone what al men thenketh
wt the lerkward that a wil the wynd ys a redy
to blowe or to be stille or to brethy softe
and alle the water of thys world welde in his glove
he hath fyue wt oute that ys foes to kenne
Eche day nat do thing that he defendeth
The fest for fere ys fayn to folwen ys wille
Dar no ste steren hym ne stemo a yeyn ys defense
I haue no tome to telle how the tour ys y maked
Alle the wryghtes at wyndelesore couthe wyrche such an oth'
ne alle the masonnes of this londe make there a fframe
The brygge hatte byde wel the bet may the spede
Uch piler ys of penaunce y polsched ful smethe
Grace hatte the gate ward a good man for sothe
his man hatte amende yow many man hym knoweth
Telleth hym this tokene trewthe wot the sothe
y performed the penaunce the prest me enioyned
and ful sory of my synnes and so schal y euere
when y thenke there on thow y were a pope
Byddeth amende yow meken hym to ys maystre
ones to wayne vp the wyket that the wenche schutte
Tho Adam and Eue heten ere bane
ffor he hath the keye and the cliket thow the kyng slepe
and yif grace graunte the to go in this wise
thou schalt y se trewthe hym self walle sitten in thyn herte
and leren the for to loue and ys lawe holde
at be y war thanne of wrath the nat that wykede schrewe
ffor he hath enuye the hym that in thyn herte sitteth
and poketh forth pryde to preyse thy selue
The boldenesse of thy bienfet maketh the blynd thenne
and so worst thow dryue out as deugh and dore y closed
y kayed and y cletaked to kepe the wyth oute
and happely an hundred wynter ar thow eft entre

Thus myght thow lesen þe loue in leking of a wench
Ac gete hit ayayn thorw grace ac thorw no gyft elles

Passus septimus

This were a wel wyked way but who haues a gyde
That myght folew vs vch foot for to we were thare
Qd perkyn the plowman be seint poule of rome
I haue an halue aker to ere by the heye way
Haued y hered that halue aker and y sowed hit after
And schal wende wt yow tyl the haye were
This were a long lettyng qd a lady in a sclayre
What scholde we wymmen wyrch the whyle
Somme schal sowe the sak for schedyng of the whete
And wyues that han wolle wyrche hit faste
And spynneth hit spedlych spare nat youre fyngres
But yf he eny halyday or eny holy eue
Loketh forth youre lynnen and laboreth thare on faste
The nedy and the naked nymeth hede how he ligeth
Casteth hem clothes for cold for so comaundeth trewthe
For y schal lene hem lif lode but yf the lond fayle
As longe as y lyue for our lordes loue of heuene
And ye louelyche ladyes wt youre longe fyngres
That ye haue selk and sendel to sowen whan tyme ys
Chesibles for chapeleynes chyrches to honoure
And al manere men that by the mete libbeth
Helpeth hym wyrche wyghtlyche that wynneth youre fode
By crist qd a knyght tho thow kennest vs the best
Ac on the teme trewly taught was y neuere
Ac kenne me qd the knyght and be crist y wyl lere
By seint poul qd perkyn for thow proferest the so lowe
Y schal swynken and sweten and sowe for vs bothe
And eke labour for youre loue al my lif tyme
In couenaunt that ye kepe holy kyrke and my self
Fro wastours and wyked men that wolde me destruye
Meyntene me yf yow myght fro al manere schrewes
And go hunte hardely the hares and the foxes
The bukkes and bores that breken myn egges
And feteth hom faukones fowles to kille
For these cometh crofte and croppeth my whete
Courteslyche the knyghte thenne comsed thes wordes
By my power perkyn y plyghte the my trewthe
To fulfille this forward for euere more here after
Ye and yut a poynt qd perkyn y prey the more
Loke thow tene no tenaunt but yf trewthe wyl assente
And thow pore me profre yow presaunt and yfel
Nyme nat a nawntre thow mow hyt nat desserue
Thenne schalt thow yelden hit a yeyen at one yeres ende
In a ful perilouse place that purgatorie hatte
And mysbede nat thy bond men the bet schalt thow spede
Loke thow be trewe of thy tonge and tales that thow hate.

Butt yf yt be of wysdom or wyt thy werkmen to chaste
yf none harlotes thyn here ne thyn holde clothys
bute hit be mynstrales or messageres that gode notes cunne
I assente by seynt Jame sayde the knyght thenne
for to wyrche by thy word whyle my lyf dureth
Perkyn apayles hym in pylgrimes wyse
& caste on his clothes y clouted for the colde
ys cokeres and ys coffus for clumse of ys fyngres
And myn hatte on myn heued y haue no betere scrippe
a bosshel of bred corn brynge me therynne
for y wil sowe hit my silf and sethen wil y wende
and ho so helpeth me to holde or egge hit myd the harwe
Or wer a wey the foules whyle the sed groweth
Schal haue leue by oure lord to lese here in heruest
and beren hit forth to his bern as baldely as my silf
Dame worche wan tyme ys ys wyf highte
and ys doughter highte do ryt so or thy dame schal the bete
ys sone hyght sewe myn of fore sleuth nat the leste
kepe vch mannes corn as thow kepest myn owne
Lothe here gras and here god or by god thow schalt a begge
lat nat thyne handes be y holed harneys to pyke
ne ly nat to do me lawghe for y louede hit neuere
for now y am hold and hor and haue of myn owne
To penaunce as a pylgrime y wyl passe wt this other
ther for y wyl or y wend do wryte my byqueste
In dei nomine amen y make hit my sylf
he schal haue my sowle tha beste hath deserued
and defenden hit fro the fend for so y byleue
Tyl he come and acounte as my crede telleth
at domes day to do me dwelle wt my sowle in his blisse
for that y labored in ys lawe al my lyf tyme
The kyrke schal haue my caroyne and kepe my bones
for of my catel and my corn a craued my tythe
y payed hit hym prestly for pel of my sowle
and he his holdyng y hope to haue me in his masse
and menegge in his memorie a mong gode sowles
My wyf schal haue that y wan wt trewthe and no more
and dele a mong my doughtres and my dere chyldren
for thow y deye to day my dettes ys y quited
I bar hom that y borwed er y to bedde yede
and wt the residewe and the remanaunt that ryghtfullyche y wonne
y wil wyrschepe there wt trewthe as long as y leue
and be ys pilegrym at the plow for poremen sake
My plow pote schal be my pik to puth a to the rot
That acumbren my colter as cammokes and wedes
Now ys Perkyn and the pylgrimes to the plow faren
To heryen this halfacre holpen hym monye
Dykeres and deluares diged vp the balkes
Ther wt was Perkyn a payed and preysed hem faste
Other werkmen there were that wroughte ful yerne.

vch man in his manere made hym silf to done
For to plese perkyn perus ful monye
At heye prime peers let þe plowh stande
And ouer sey hem hym silf ho so best wroughte
Scholde ben huyred þer aftur when heruest tyme come
Thenne sete summe and songe at þe nale
And holpe erye þe half acre with hey trollilolly
By þe prynse of paradis quod peers in his wrath
But ye arise þe rather and rapen yow to werch
Schal no greyn that here groweth gladye yow at nede
ne y nol leue yow no lyflode nouther loef ne cake
ne no skynes corn by crist that in my crofte groweth
And thaw ye deye for deul þe deuel haue that recch
Thenne were faytores a ferd and fayned hem blynde
Summe leyde here legges a lyry as such losels conneth
And pleyneden to peers with such pitouse wordes
We han no lymes to labore with lord y graced bethe
ac we preyen for yow peers and for youre plow also
That god for his grace youre greyn multeplie
And yelde yow youre almesse that ye yeuen vs here
For we mowe neyther swynke ne swete such sikenesse vs eyleth
ȝyf hit be soth that ye seyen y schal sone aspye
ye ben wastores y wot wel trewthe wot þe sothe
And y am his holde hyne and oughte hym to warne
Whiche wastores in world his werkmen distruyeth
ye eten that they scholde ete that swynketh for vs alle
Ac trewthe schal techen yow his teme for to dryue
Bothe to sette and to sowe and to sauen his tylthe
Cacch kowes fro his corn kepen his bestes
Or ye schal eten barly bred and of þe brok drynke
But yf he blynd or broke schanked or bedreden ligge
They schal ete as good as y so me god helpe
Tyl god of his grace gare hem to ryse
Ankeres and heremytes that holdeth hem in here selles
Schal haue of myn almesse al þe whyle y libbe
ynowh ech day at noon and no more after
Leste his flessh and þe feend foulede his soule
Ones at noon ys ynowh that no werk ne haunteth
A byt wel þe bettre that bummeth nat ofte
Thenne gan wastor to wrathen hym and wolde haue y foughte
And to peers þe plowman profered his glove
A bretoner a braggere a bosted hym also
And bad hym go pisse with his plowh pynysche schrewe
Wolle yow nelle yow we wille han oure wille
And bothe thy flour and thy flessh fecch whan we liketh
And maken vs merye ther myd maugre thy chekes
Thenne peers þe plowman pleyned hym to þe knyghte

To kepen him as couenaunt was fro cursede schrewes
Fro wastoures that wayte wynneres to schende
Curteysliche the knyghte thenne as his kynde wolde
Warned Wastor and wissed him bettre
Or thow schalt abigge by the lawe by the ordre that y were
I was nat wonyd to werche now wil y nat bygynne
And let lighte of the lawe and lasse of the knyghte
And counted peres at a pese and his plowh bothe
And manesed him and his men to mysdon hem aftsones
Now by the peril of my soule y schal apeyre yow alle
And houped aftir hunger that herd him at the furste
Awreke me of thise wastoures quod peris that this worlde schenden
Hunger in haste thenne hente wastor by the mawe
And wrong him so by the wombe that al watred his eyen
And buffeted the bretoner aboute the chekes
That he loked lik a lanterne al his lyf aftir
He bete hem so bothe that he barst nere here guttes
Ne hadde peris with a pese lof preyed hunger to leue
And with a benes batte ayede hem bytwene
And hitte hunger ther mydde that alle his guttes swolle
And bledde in to the body ward a bolle ful of growel
Ne hadde eyr furst the fysyk y for what tho same
So a bake the barly bred and benes that they eten
They haued be ded be this day and dolven al warme
Faytoures for fere tho flowen in to bernes
And flapten on with flayles fro morwen tyl euen
Beynge barly breed and water
That hunger was nat hardy on hem for to loke
For a potte ful of peses that peris had ymaked
An hep of heremytes hente hem spades
And dolven dykes and dunge to ditten out hunger
Blynde and bedredun were botned a thousend
That hadde be blynde and broke legges be the heye weye
Hunger hem heled with an hote cake
And lame men lymes were lythed that tyme
And be comen knaues to kepe mennes bestes
And preyed par charite with peris for to dwelle
Al for couetyse of his corn to chace awey hunger
And peris was proude therof and putte hem to maystry
And yaf hem mete and moneye as they myghte disserue
Thenne haued peris pite and preyed hunger to wende
Hom in to his owne erd and halde there euere
At yit y preie the quod peris ar thow passe forther
Of beggares and bydderes what best be to done
For y woot wel be thow went they wil worche ful ille
Meschyf hit makith they ben so meke nouthe

and for defaute of fode thys folke they wyrchen
and ȝit ben my blody brethryne for god boughte vs
alle Treuthe taughte me ones to louey hem vch one
to helpe hem of alle thing as they han neede
now wolde y wyte yf thow wist what were the beste
how y myghte amaystren hem and maken he to wyrche
the that ben stalewore and stronge and styuores bath holden
for beggeren and blynde and broke legges wyrches
that ben syke and sory y schal y do my silf
that they haue bred and brede beddyng and clot
and kepe hem fro colde so me crist helpe
and eke fro hung and shame as myn owne childre
herke now qd hung and holde hit for a wysdom
bolde beggares and bygge that mow here bred by swynke
wt howndes bred and horse bred holde vp here hertes
a bate hem wt benes for bollyng of here wombe
and yf the gromes gruch bidde hem go and swynke
and he schal soupe swetter when he it hath disserued
and yf yt be eny frekes fortune haue a peyred
wt fuyr or wt fals men fonde such to knowe
Conforte hym wt thy catel for crystes loue of heuene
loue hem and laue hem and so lawe of kynde wolde
J wolde nat greue god qd piers for al the god that y welde
myghte y synneles do as thow seyst seyde piers theime
ye y by hote god qd hung or elles the bible lyes
go to genesis the geaunt engendrour of vs alle
In swoore and swynk yow schalt thy mete telye
and laboren for thy lyf lode and so oure lord hyghte
and sapience seith the same y say hit in the byble
piger pre frigus no felde nolde tilye
a schal go begge and bydde and no man bete ys hung
matheu wt the mannes face mowtheth these wordes
that Seruus nequam haue a mnam and for a nolde hit vse
he haued maugre of ys mayster for euer more after
and by nam hym ys mnam for a nolde wyrche
and yaf yt hym in haste that hadde ten there by fore
and sethe he seyde that ys seruant hit herde
he that hath schal haue to helpe there hym neeth
and he that nawght hath schal nawght haue ne no man hy helpe
and that he weneth wel to haue y wyl hit hym by reue
Of thys mater y myght make a longe tale
ac hit falleth nat for me for y am no dekne
to preche the peple what that poynt menes
kynde wyt wolde that euery wyght wroughte
or to teche or to telle or trauayle wt handes
Contemplatyf lyf or actyf lyf crist wolde hit also
the sawter seyt in salme in beati omnes
labores manuum tuarum quia manducabis

Yis best y blessed of god ant the bet schalt thou spede
ȝut y preye the qd peres porcharite ant thou cunne
any lef of leche craft lere hit me y bydde
for y haue summe seruans ben sike other whyle
Of al the woke they wyrche nat so here wombe aketh
I wot wel qd hunger what sykenesse hem ayleth
They han maunged ouer muche that maketh hem to grone
ant eke y dronke to depe that doth hem harme ofte
Ac y hote the qd hunger as thou thyn hele wilnest
That thou drynke no day ar thou dyne sum what
Ette nat y hote ar hunger the bydde
ant sende of ys sauce to sauere wt thy lippes
ant kep sum for to soper tyme ant sitte nat to longe
a ryse vp ar thyn appetyte haue ete ys fulle
lat nat syre sorfet sitte at thy borde
lef nat that lyere for he ys licorus of tunge
ant aftr many maneres metes ys mawe ys a hungred
ant yf thou diete the thus y dar legge myn eres
That fisik schal ys furred hodus for ys fode sille
ant eke ys cloke of calabre wt the knappes of golde
ant be fayn by my fayth ys fysyk to lete
ant lerne to labore wt land for liflode ys swete
I defame nat fysyk for the science ys gode
Ac sum cunynge kaytyues that kunnen nat rede a lettere
maketh hem maysters men for to hele
At hit ar maysters morthrares men for to quelle
ant none leches but lyares lord hem amende
In ecclesiastico the clerc that can rede ~~may se hit there hym self~~
May se hit there hym self ant senes teche other
Honora medicum he seyt for necessitate
For helthe from heuene y hope doth out springe
ant there for the byble hit ant in ys bok techet
That leches of lorens scholde here lower haue
a regibus & principibus erit merces eorum
Of princes ant prelat here pencyon schal a ryse
ant of no pore peple no penelworth gode take
Ac lewed lumbardes londona han a ryued
That gloten ys a god there ant greueth me fil ofte
ant maketh hem maystres ant medecynes schapeth
ant casteth men of the caroyacle in to the kyrke yerd
fflemmynges ant frenche men ant fele of this englysch
Be seynt pernele qd peres me payeth wel your wordes
This ys a louely lesson lord hit the for yelde
Wende now whan thy wille ys that wel the by tyde
I be hote the qd hunger that hennes nolly wende
Tyl y haue dyned by thys day ant y drunke bothe
Thenne haues peres no peny pullett to bigge
noyther gos ne grys but to grene chesus
a wel a potteful of wey ant welles croddes
a lof of benes ant bran to bake among myn hens

ant suche a swer by ye soule he ne had no salt bakon
ne no kokenay by crist colopp' to make
I. haue persile ant poret ant many plat koules
ant eke a kow ant a calf ant a cart mare
to drawe a. feld dunge while the drugthe lasteth
ant by thys lyflode y. mot liue til lammasse tyme
ant by that y hope to haue heruest in my crofte
Thenne may y. dyghten thy dyner as me dere liketh
alle the pore peple thenne pese coddes fetten
benes ant bake apples they broughten in here lappe
Chiboll' ant cheruilles ant chiries ful ripe
ant profreden thys present to plese wyth hungir
hungir ete this in haste ant axed after more
Thenne the folk for fere fetten hym monye
grene porett ant pesis to peyse hym for euer
By that yt neyghed nere heruest that newe corn cam to chepinge
Thenne was folk fayn ant fedde hungir wyth the beste
Wt gode ale ant glotonye geten hym to slepe
ant tho nolde wastor nat werche but wandren a-boute
ne no beggare eten bred that benes in come
but yt were koket or clermatyn or of clene whete
ne none halpeny ale in eny wyse drynke
But of the best ant the brownest that in borwe ys to selle
laborers that han no land bot liue on here handes
deyneden to day of nyghte olde wort'
May no peny ale hem plese ne no pese of bakon
But yt be fresch flesch or fissh fryed other bake
ant that chaud or pluschaud for chillyng of ye mawe
ant thowe he be fed wt fresch mete ant of the fynest drynke
but he be heyliche y. hyred elles wol he gruche
That he was werkman y. wrought warien the tyme
ant thenne corsen the kyng ant al the counsayl after
Such lawes to loke laborers to chaste
ac whyle hungir was here mayster wolde non gruch ~~ne stryue~~
ne stryue a. yeyn ye statut so sternelyche a. loked
ac war ye wel werkmen wynneth while ye mowe
ffor hungir hyderward hasteth hym faste
he schal a. wake wt water wastours to chaste
er. fyf yer be ful fild such famyn schal a. rise
Thorw flod ant thorw foul wedir frutes schulle fayle
ant so seyth Catun ant sent yow to warne

Passus Octauus

Trewthe herde telle here of ant to perus sente
to taken ys teme ant telyen ye the
ant purchased hym a pardoun a pena & a culpa
for hym ant for hys ayres for eu more after
ant bad hym halden hym at hom ant heryen ys leyes
ant alle that hym holpe to herye or to sowe.

or eny manere mestere that myght peres helpe
part of that pardoun the pope hath y graunted,
kyngis and knyghtis that kepen holi kirke
and ryghtfulliche in rewmes reulen the peple
han pardoun thorw purgatorie to passe ful sone
in paradys wyth patriarkis to pleyen there after
bisshopis y blessed that bothe lawes connthe
lokun on that one lawe leren men that other
and bereth hem bothe on here bak as here baner scheweth
prechen here persons the perils of synne
hou that schabbed schep schal here wolle saue
han pardoun wyth the apostlis when they passe hennes
and at the day of dome at here deys sitte
marchauntis in the margyne hauen many yeres
but no pena & a culpa the pope nolde hem graunte
for they helde nat here halydayes as holy chyrche wolde
and for they swere by here soule and so most god hem helpe
ayens clene consciens here catel to selle
ac under ys secrete sel treuthe sente hem a lettre
that they scholde bygge baldely what hem beste liked,
and sillen hit sone ayeyn and sauen here wynnyngis
and maken mesondeux therewith myseyse men to help
wykede weyes wyghtlich to amende
and beten briggis a boute that to broke were
marien maydenes or maken hem nonnes
pore wydewes that wylned be wedded no more
fynden hem fode for lordus loue of heuene
sette scoleres to scole or to som skynnes craftes
releuen religioun and renten hem bettere
y schal sende you my self seynt myhel myn angel
that no deuel schal you dere deye wan ye schull
that he ne schal sende youre soule sauf in to heuene
and by fore the face of my fader fourme youre sete
vsurerye and auarice and othes y defende
and that no gyle go wyth you but the grayth treuthe
thenne were marchauntis mery many wopen for ioye
and yeuen wille for this wrytyng wollen clothes
ffor he copied thus here clause couth hym gret mede
men of lawe hauen lest for lettered they ben alle
and so seyth the sauter and sapience bothe
Sup innocentem munera non accipies; a regibus & principibus erit merces eorum
of pryncis and prelatis youre pencioun schal a ryse
ac of no pore peple no peneworth schal ye take
ac that spendeth ys speche and speketh for the pore
that ys innocent and nedy and no man apeyreth
conforteth hym in that cas coueyteth nat ys godis
and for oure lordes loue lawe for hym scheweth
schal no deuil at ys deth day dere hym a myte
that he ne worth sicur sauf and so the sauter witnesseth
ac to bygge water ne wynde ne wit ys the thridde

Wolde nere holy writ god wot the sothe
thise thre for thralles ben throwe among vs alle
To waxen and to wanye where that god liketh
his pardoun in purgatorie ful petit ys y trowe
That mercede for ye motyng of menes mys resseyueth
ye legystres and lawyeres hoo yt now trowe ye
ye semes ye seth thus yow self wheth ye the beste
Alle lybbynge laborers that lyueden by here handes
That treweliche token and treweliche wonne
And lyueden in loue in lawe for here lowe hert
Hadden the same absolucioun that sent was pers
Begganeres ne byddares ne bin nat in the bulle
But yt be in the bak half wt oute by hem silue
But yf here suggestioun be soth wen they schal begge
For he that begget or byt but yf he neede haue
he ys fals wt the fend and defraudith the nedy
And eke gyleth the gyuer a geynes ys wille
thus they leuen nat ne no lawe kepen.
Were they haue halywatr or haly brede habbeth they no ware
And eke vnschryvne schrewes thyl schyrthursday at eue
They wedde none womme that they wt dele
And as wilde best wt weche worchen vp to gyderes
And bryngeth forth barnes that bastard ben holde
Or ye bak or ye boon a breketh in ye youthe
And goth and fayteth thenne wt here fauntes for euer more after
Ther ys mo mys schape among hem ho so taketh hede
Thenne of alle other maner men that on thys molde wandereth
Tho that leden thus here lyf mowen lothy the tyme
That euere they wer men wrot wen they schulle hennes fare
Ac olde men and hore that helples ben of strengthe
And womme wt childe that wyrche ne mowe
Blynde men and bedreden and broken in here membris
That taken this mischef mekelyche han as myche pardoun
As pers the plowman and yut a poynt more
Ful loue of here lownesse oure lord hem hath grauntid
Here penaunce and here purgatorye vp on thys puyr erth.

Peres qd a prest tho: þi pardon most I rede
For I wil construe eche clause: & kenne it the on englysche
And peres at his preyer: the pardon unfoldede
Et qui bona egerunt in vitam eternam qui vero mala in ignem eternum
In two lynes it lay: & not a letter more
And was wryten ryth thus: in wyttenisse of treuthe
Peter qd the prest tho: I can no pardon fynde
But do wel & haue wel: & god schal haue þi soule
And do euyl & haue euyl: hope thow non oder

What after thi deth day . to helle schalt thow wende
And peirs for pure tene . pulledyt a sunder and seyde
Si ambulauo in medio umbre mortis no timebo mala qm tu mecu
I schal sesin of my sowyng . and swynke not so harde
Ne aboute my lyflode . so besi be no more
Off preyeris and penans . my plow schal ben here after
And be lowry þt I be low . or my lyf lode fayle
þe prophete his payn ete . in penaunce and wepyng
Be þt the sawter us seyth . so dede many othyr
ffuerunt m[i]chi lacrime mee panes die ac nocte
What lovyth god wely . his lyflode is wol mete
And but if luk lye he lernyt us anothyr . be fowlys þt we ne scholde
So besy be aboute . to make the wombe joye
Ne solliciti sitis . he seyth in his gospel
And schewyth be exsample ousself for to wysse
The fowlys in the firmamet . who fynt he in wynter
Whan the frost fresyth . fode hem be howyth
Have þei no fode to go to . but god fynyth he alle
What quod þe prest to perkyn . petyr as me thynkyt
Thow art lettryth alytil . who lernede the on boke
Abstinence the abysse . myn a b c me tawthe
And concience cam after ward . and kennyd me bettyr
Were þu a prest quod he . thow mytist preche whan þu lykede
Quod licturam no cognoui . þt myth be thi teme
Lewyd lorel quod he . lytil lokyst þu the bybil
Eice derisores & iurgia cu eis ne crescat
On salamons sawis . lytyl þu be holdyst
The prest and perkyn . eythyr aposid othyr
And thorow here wordist . I wok and waytede aboute
And saw þe sonne eue south . syttyn þt tyme
Meteles and moneles . on malverne hillys
Musyng on þis mater . a myle wey I zede
Many tyme þis metelis . hath mad me to stodye
And for þs lif plowman . petowsly in herte

pay

For þat I say sleppyng if it so be myȝth
Ac caton construyth nay and canonystys bothe
And seyn be hem self sompnia ne cures
Ac for þe bible beryth wyttenes wan dannyel þe prophete
Demyd the dremys of a kyng onys
That nabugodonosor nemyn þis clerkys
Dannyel seyde sere kyng thi sweuene is to mene
That unkouþe kyngis schul come þi kyngdome to cleyme
Among lowere lordis thi londis schul be departid
As dannyel demyd in dede fel it after
þe kyng lees his lordschepe and lasse me it hadde
And iosep met merueylously how þe mone & þe sonne
And the eleuene sterris halsede him alle
Beaufily quod his fader for defaut we schulle
I my self and my sonys seke þe for nede
It be fel as his fader seyde in pharaoes tyme
þat iosep was iustise egipt to kepe
Al þis makyt me mychil on metels to þinke
Many tymis at mydnyth wan I scholde slepe
On pers the plowman and which a pardon he hadde
And how þe prest inpugnit al be pure reson
And demyd þat dowel indulgense passyd
Byennalys & trienalys and bischopis letteris
Dowel at þe day of doom ys dyngneleche undirfongid
He passith al þe pardon of seynt petris chyrche
Now hat þe pope power pardon to graunt
The peple wtout ony penance to passe to ioy
This is a leef of be leue as letturid me techith
Quodcumque ligaueris sup(er) t(er)ram &c
And I be leue lely oure lord for bede ellys
þat pardon and penance & preyers to gydere
How saue soulys þat haue synnyd seuene sythis dedly
Ac to trostyn on trienalys trewly me thinkyth

Is not so seker for þe soule certys as is dowel
Where fore I rede ȝou lordis // þat riche ben on erthe
Up on trust on ȝoure tresour // trionalis to haue
Be ȝe neuer þe balder // to breke þe ten hestis
And namely ȝe maystris // meyris & iugis
That haue þe welthe of þe world // for wise men be holden
For to purchase pardon // & þe popis bullys
At þe dredful day of doom // whan dede schul arisyn
And comyn alle to fore crist // acountis to ȝelde
How þou laddist þi lif // and his lawis keptest
What þou dost day be day þe doom wil reherse
Of a pokeful of pardon ne no prouincialis letteris
Thow þou be fondyn in fraternite among þe foure ordres
And haue indulgence dobble fold but dowel helpe
I nolde ȝif for ȝoure pardon o pies hele
ffor I conseil al cristen to crien god mercy
And mary his moder be mene be twene
Þat god ȝif vs grace er we gon hennys
Swech werkys to werke wil we ben here
And after oure deth day dowel reherse
At þe doom þat we deden al as he vs bad & tawthe
And þat it so mote be to god pray we all
To vs & all cristin god leue it so be ffiat Amen

Explicit vita & visio Petri plowman